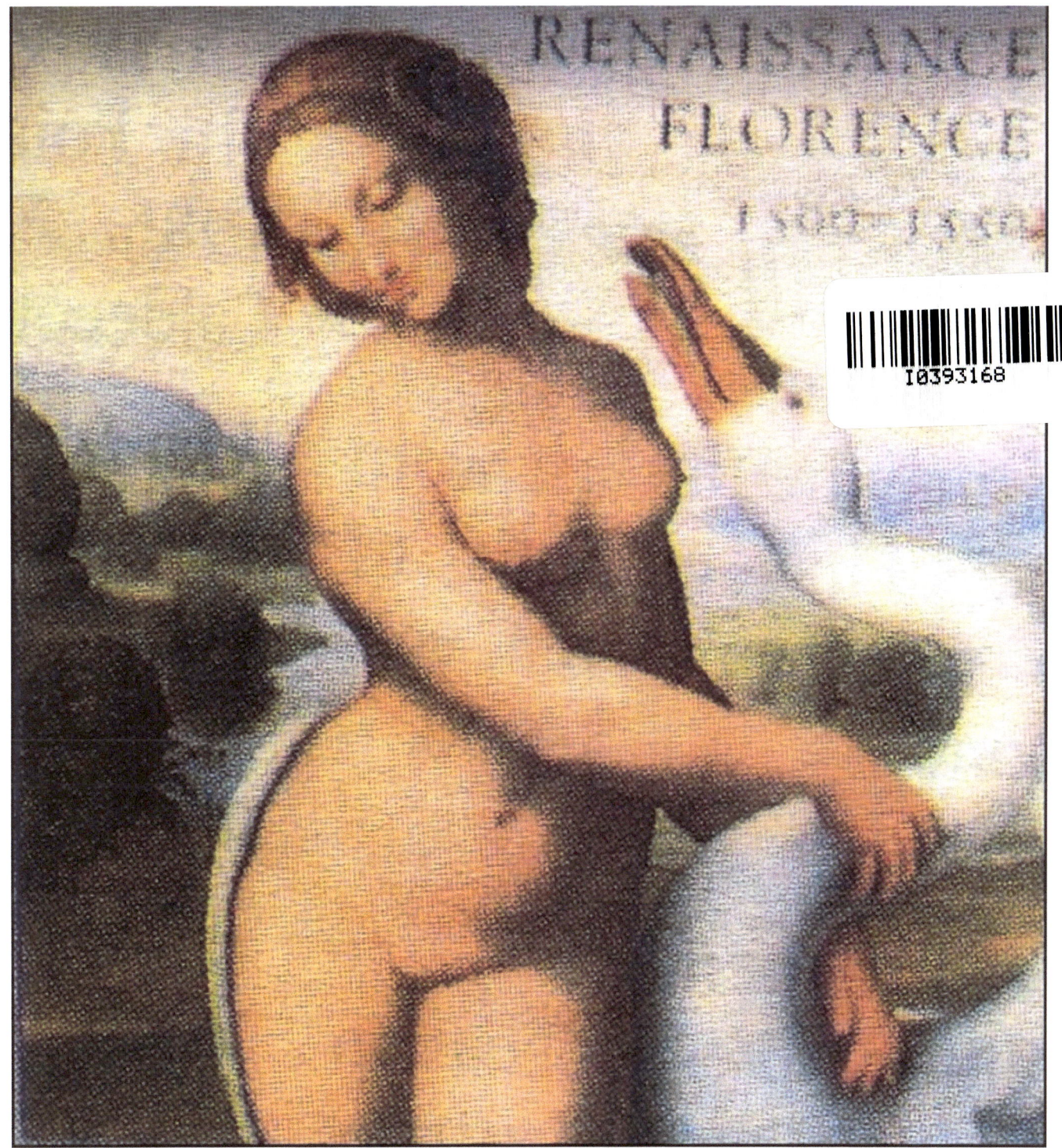

Renaissance Painting, Florence, 1500

WELCOME! We hope you enjoy this Fave Art-9 album collection of classic paintings. Most art works are copied from the internet, posters, pictures and books. Most are collector's items and can be seen in famous galleries and private homes. The originals are very expensive but copies are available from some dealers. You may display this book as coffee table book in your living room, as conversation piece. You may give this as gift . You may cut out and frame each page. Each art work is 8.5x11 inches and suitable for framing, and for wall decors.

The ISBN Code Numbers of this book are:
ISBN-13: 978- 1544112435 & ISBN-10: 1544112432
Printed in USA. Free to copy by anybody. Why copy? Just buy the book.
My other books list can be accessed at:
http://tinyurl.com/mj76ccq and http://www.jobelizes6.wix.com/mysite.
My contact email is job_elizes@yahoo.com. (Tatay Jobo Elizes, Pub.)

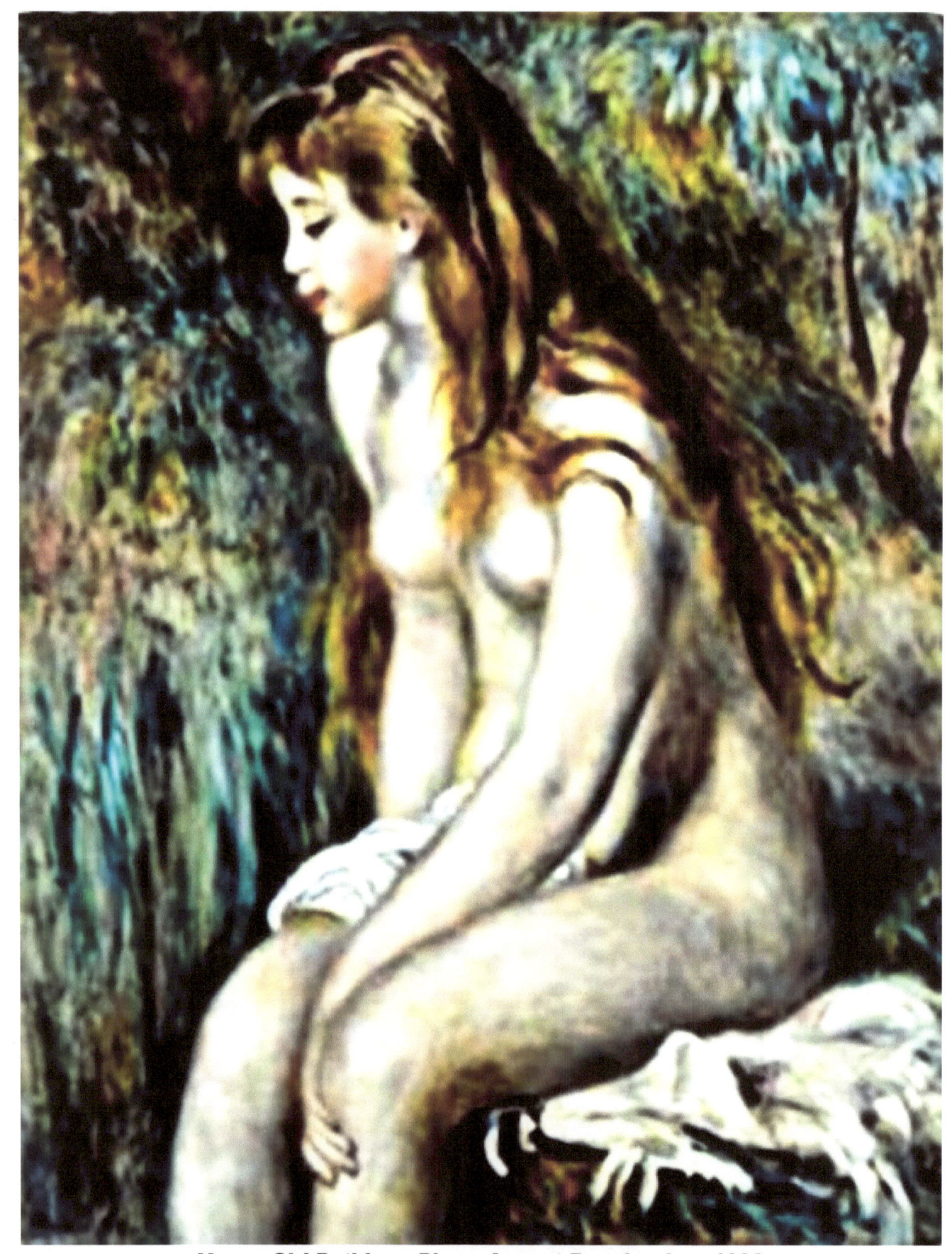

Young Girl Bathing – Pierre August Renoir, circa 1892

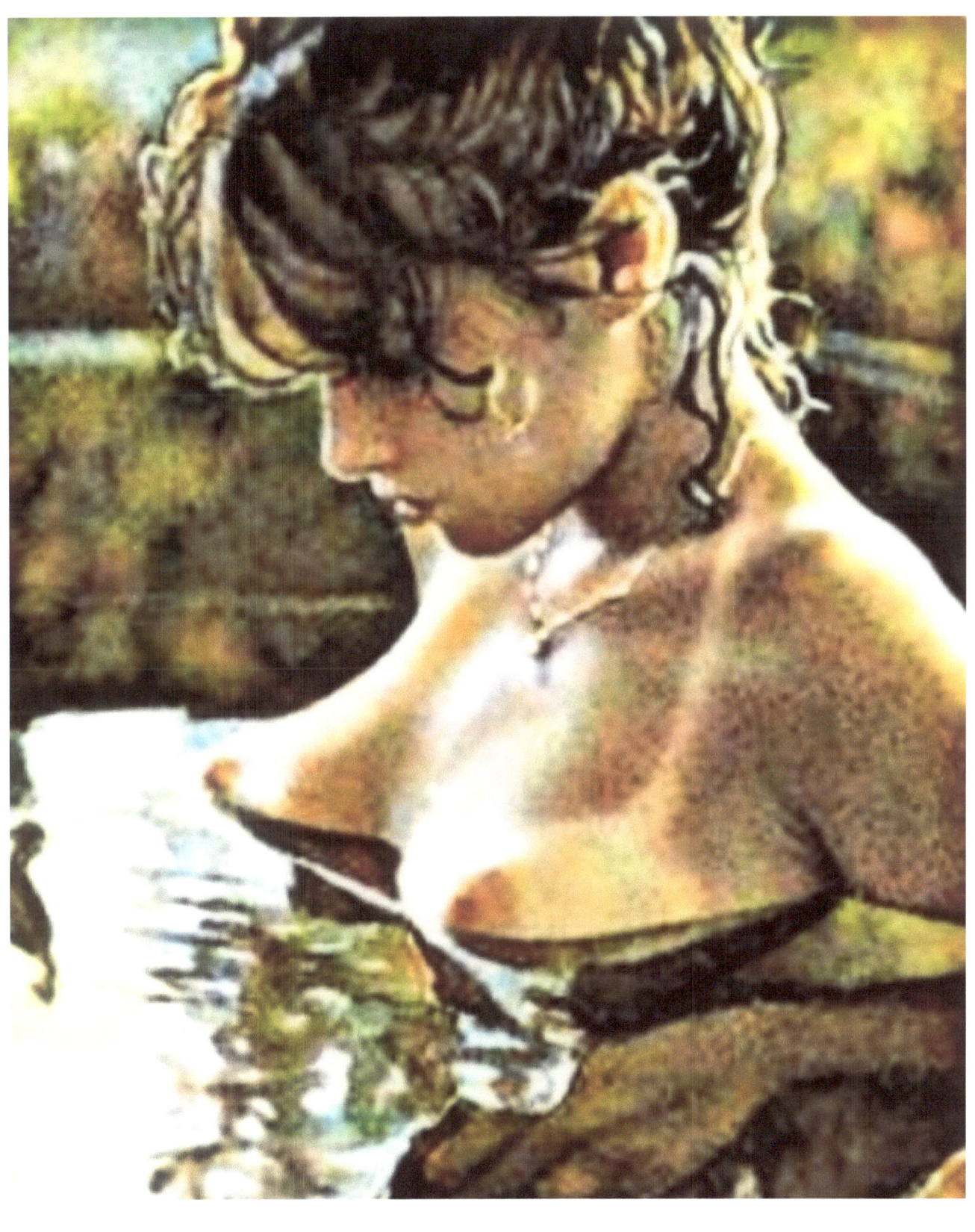

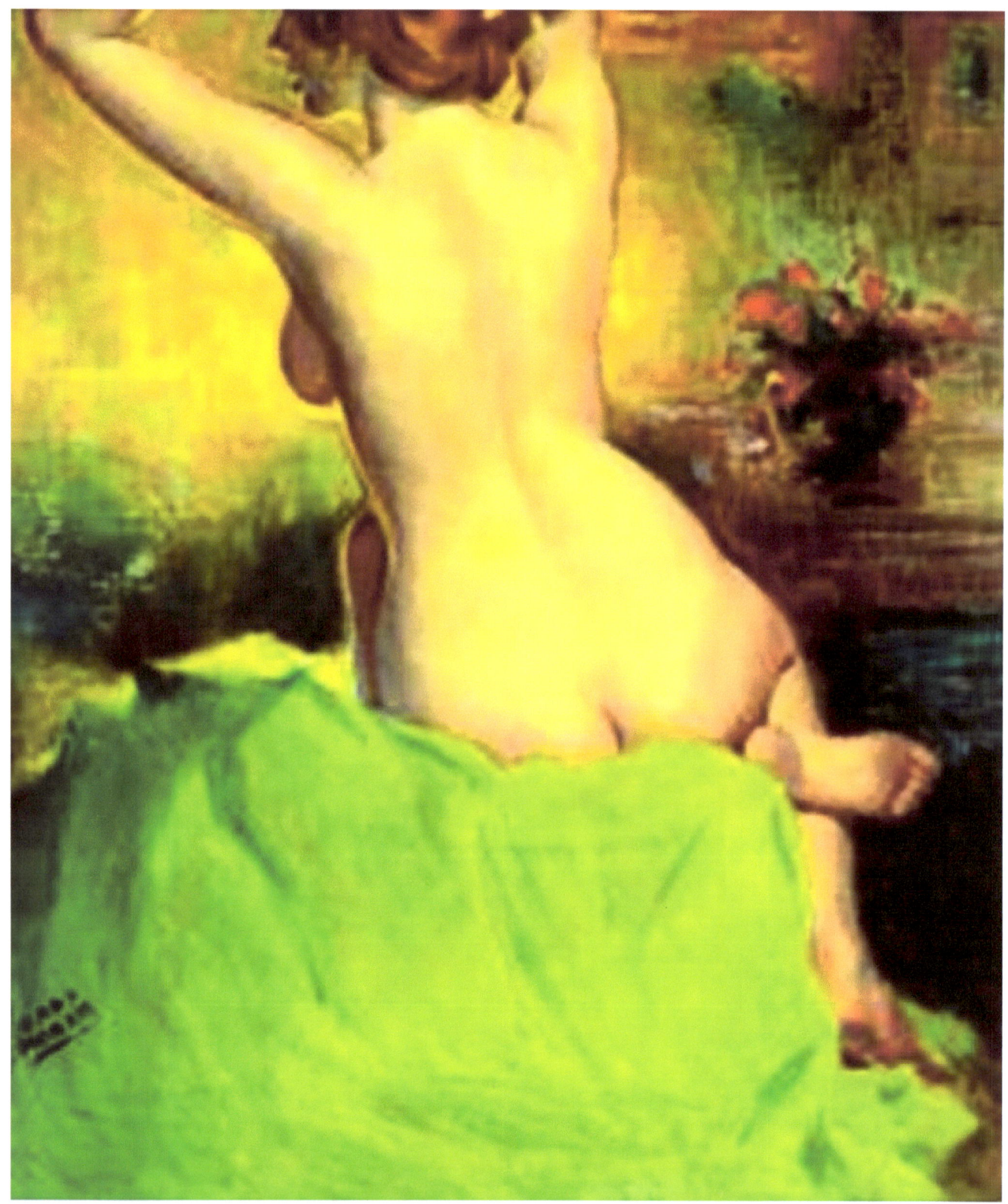

Daniel Estevez – Arte, year and artist unknown

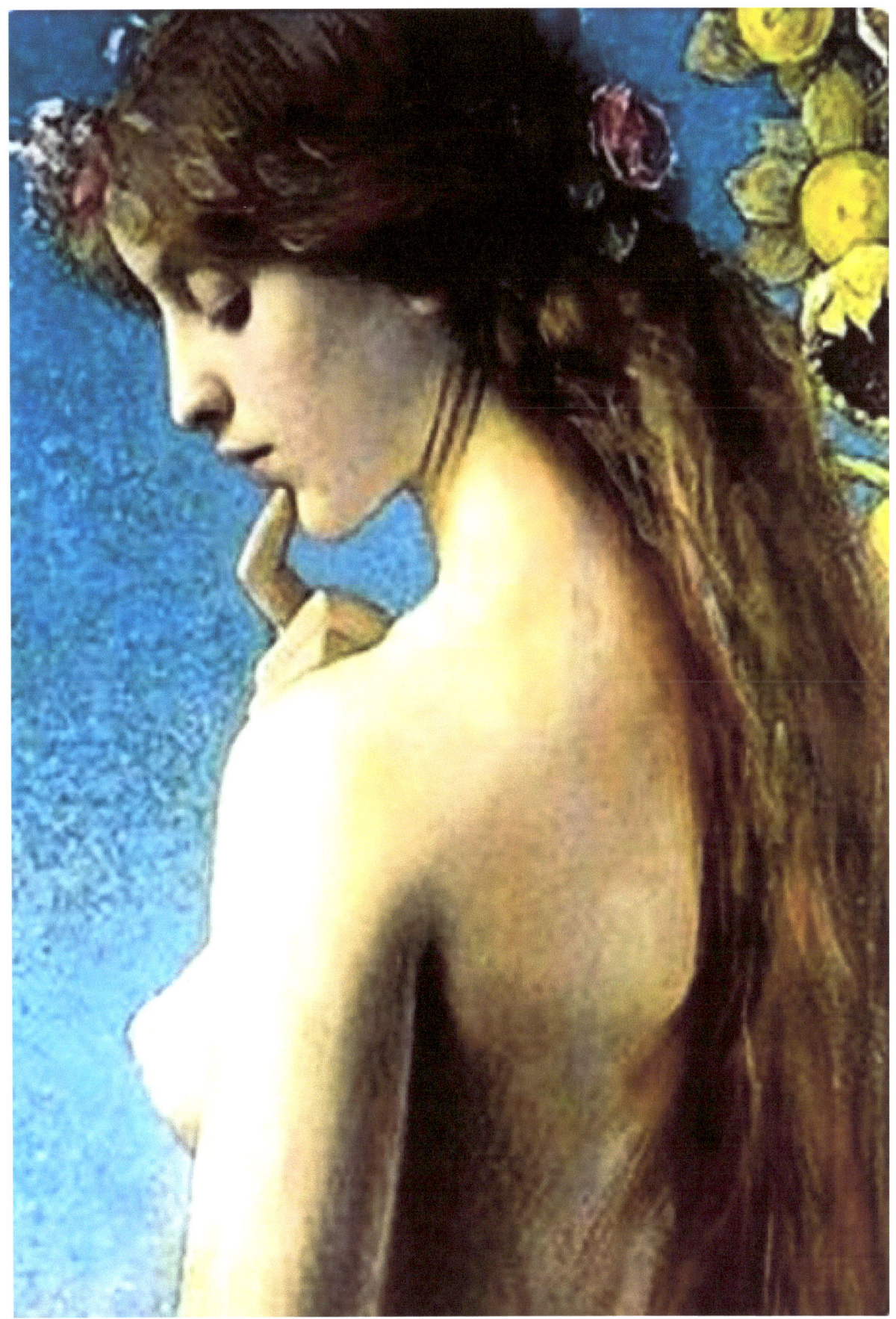

Artist Sam Carlo – year unknown

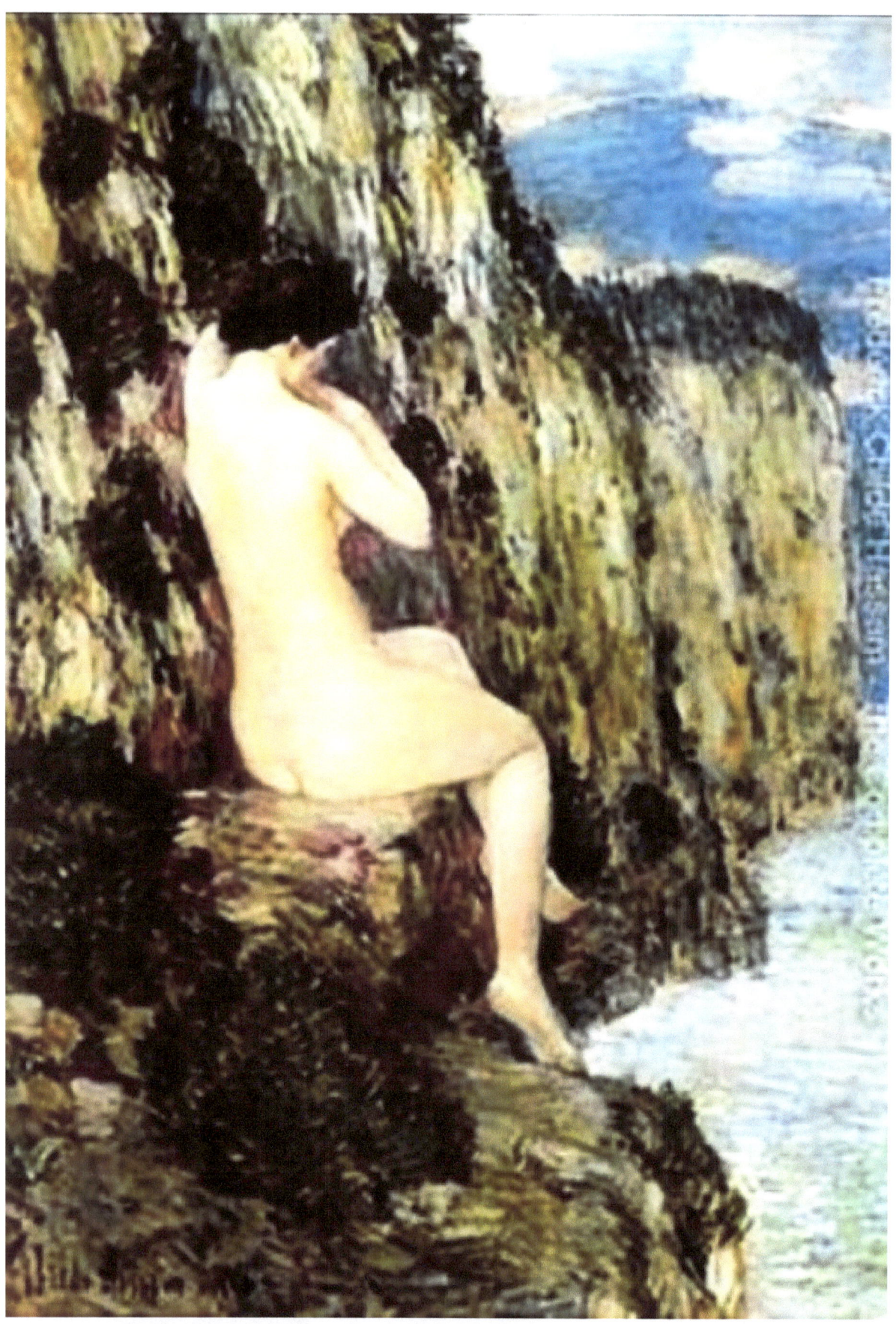

Nude on the Cliffs – Frederick Childe Hassam, Late 1800's

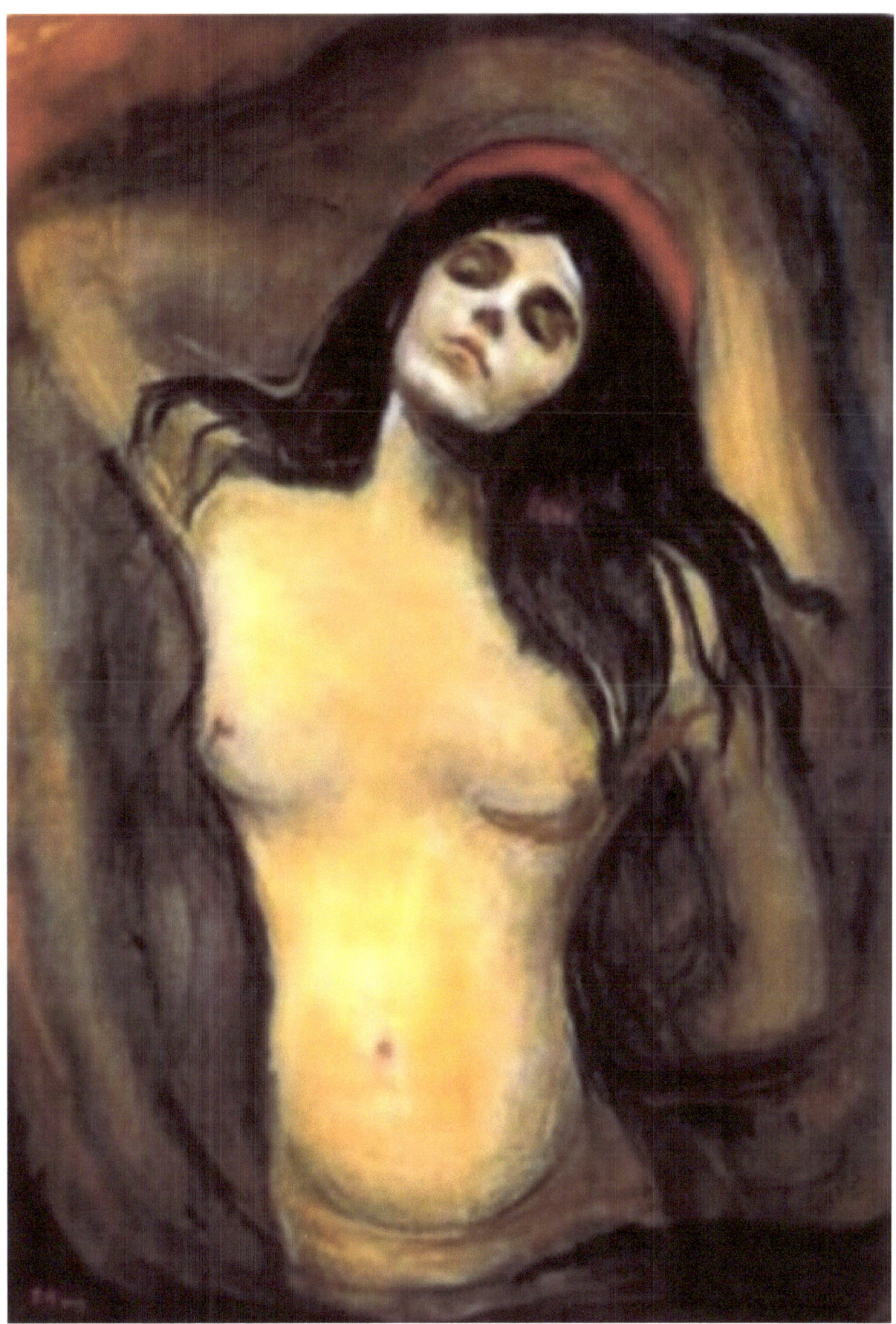

Virgin Madonna – Edvard Munch, Late 1800's

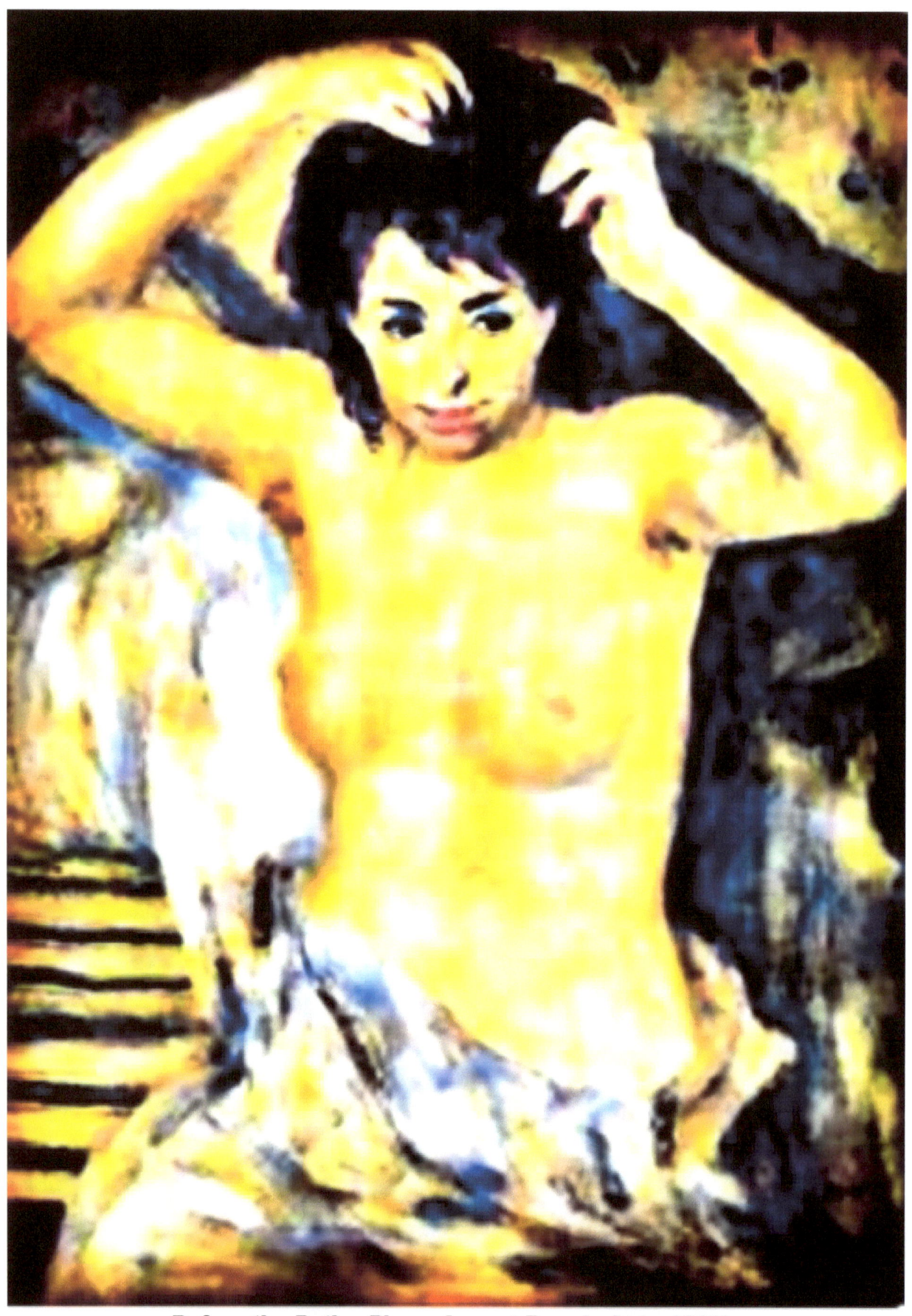

Before the Bath – Pierre August Renoir, Late 1800's

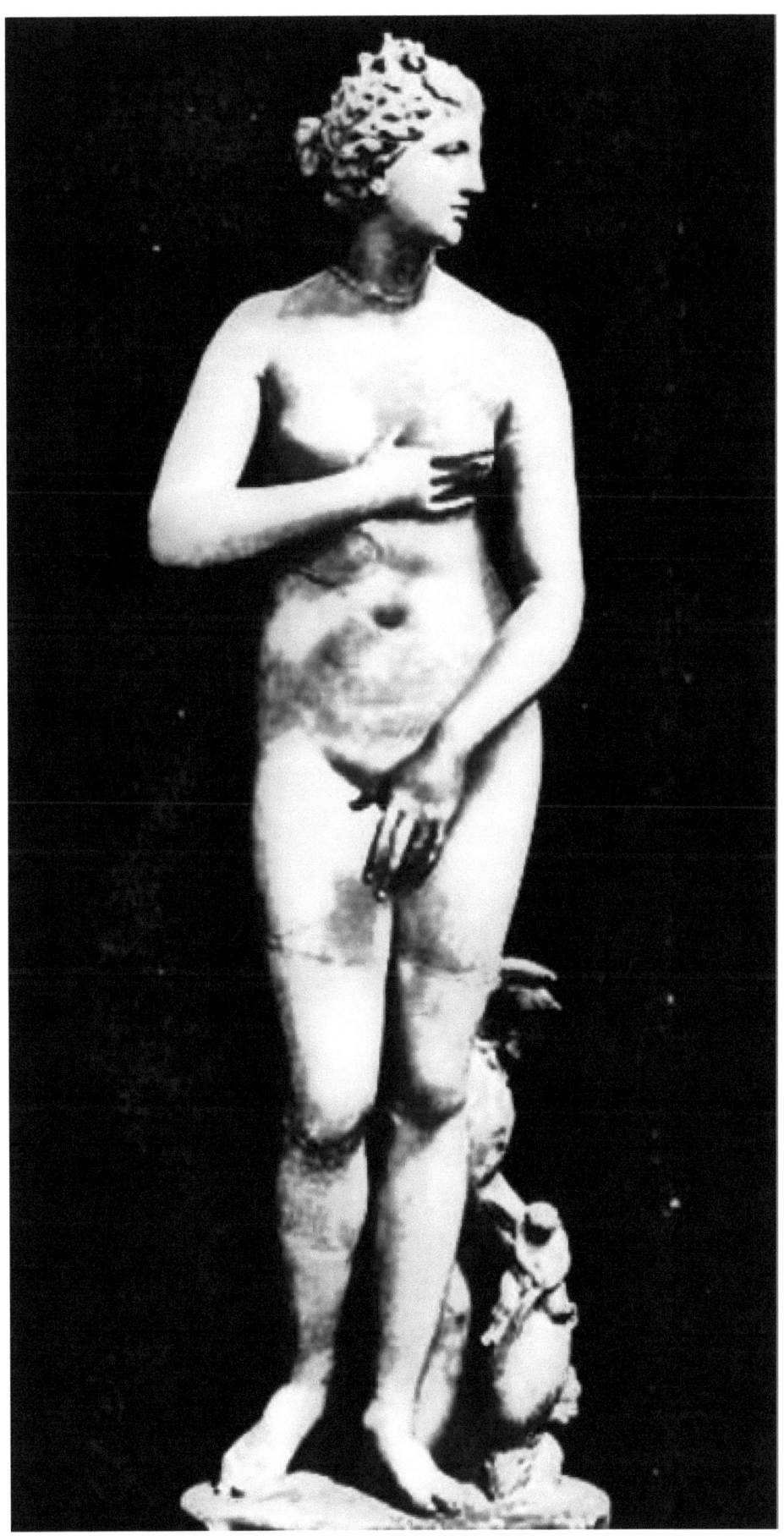

Statue of Venus

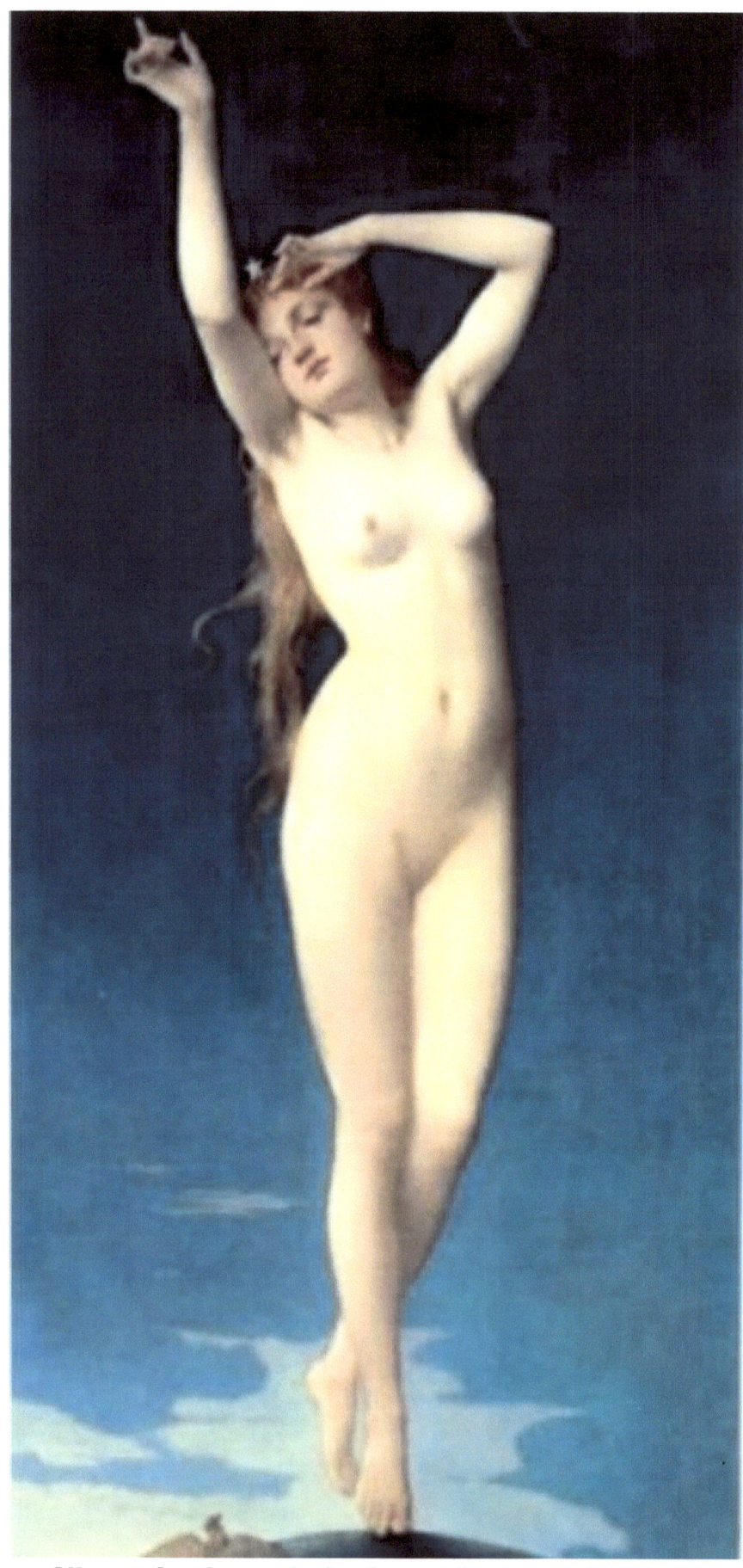

Silence for the soul – by James Bertrand, 1823 - 87

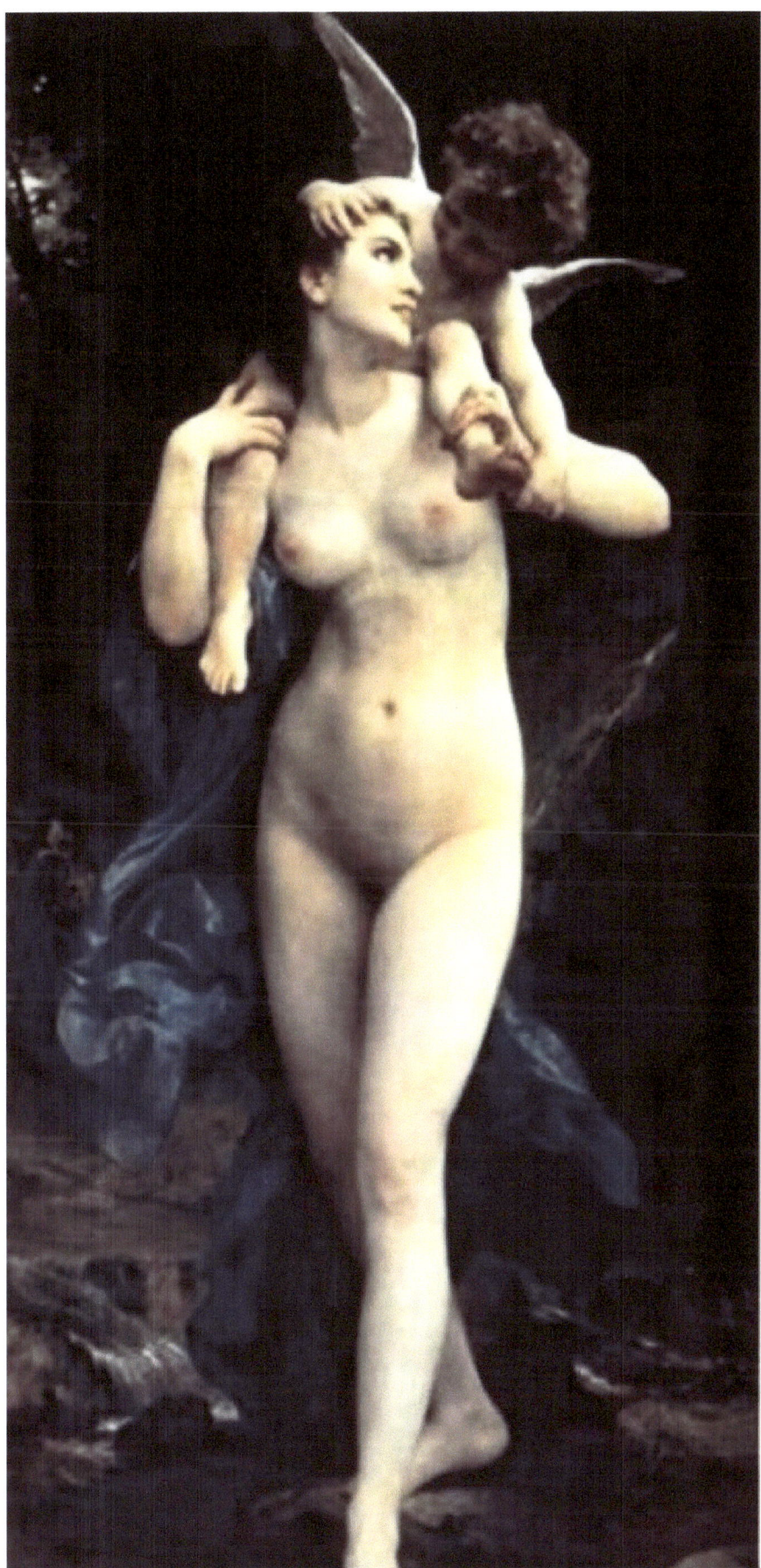

Youth and Cupid by William Bouguereau, 1877

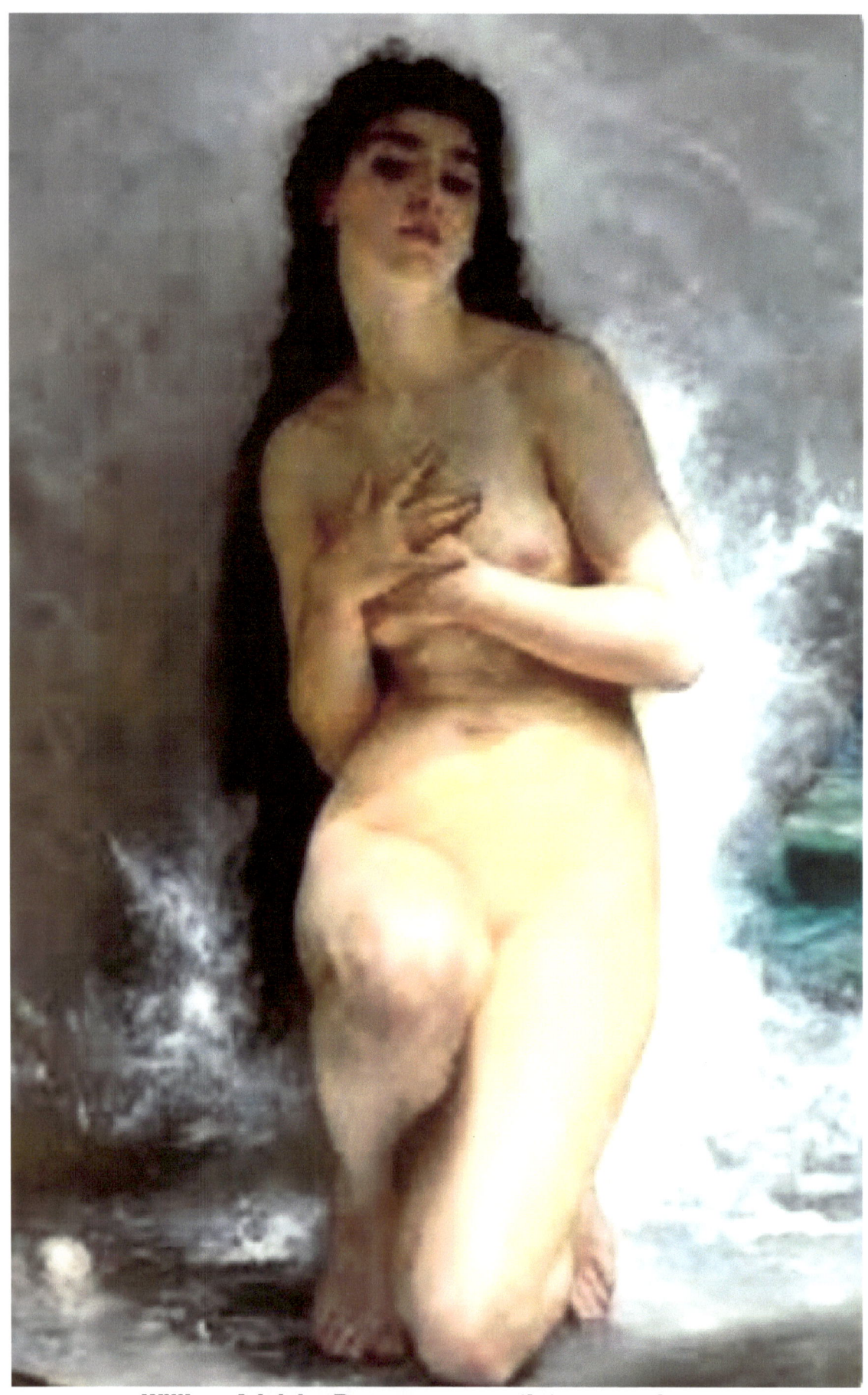

William Adolphe Bouguereau – artist, year unknown

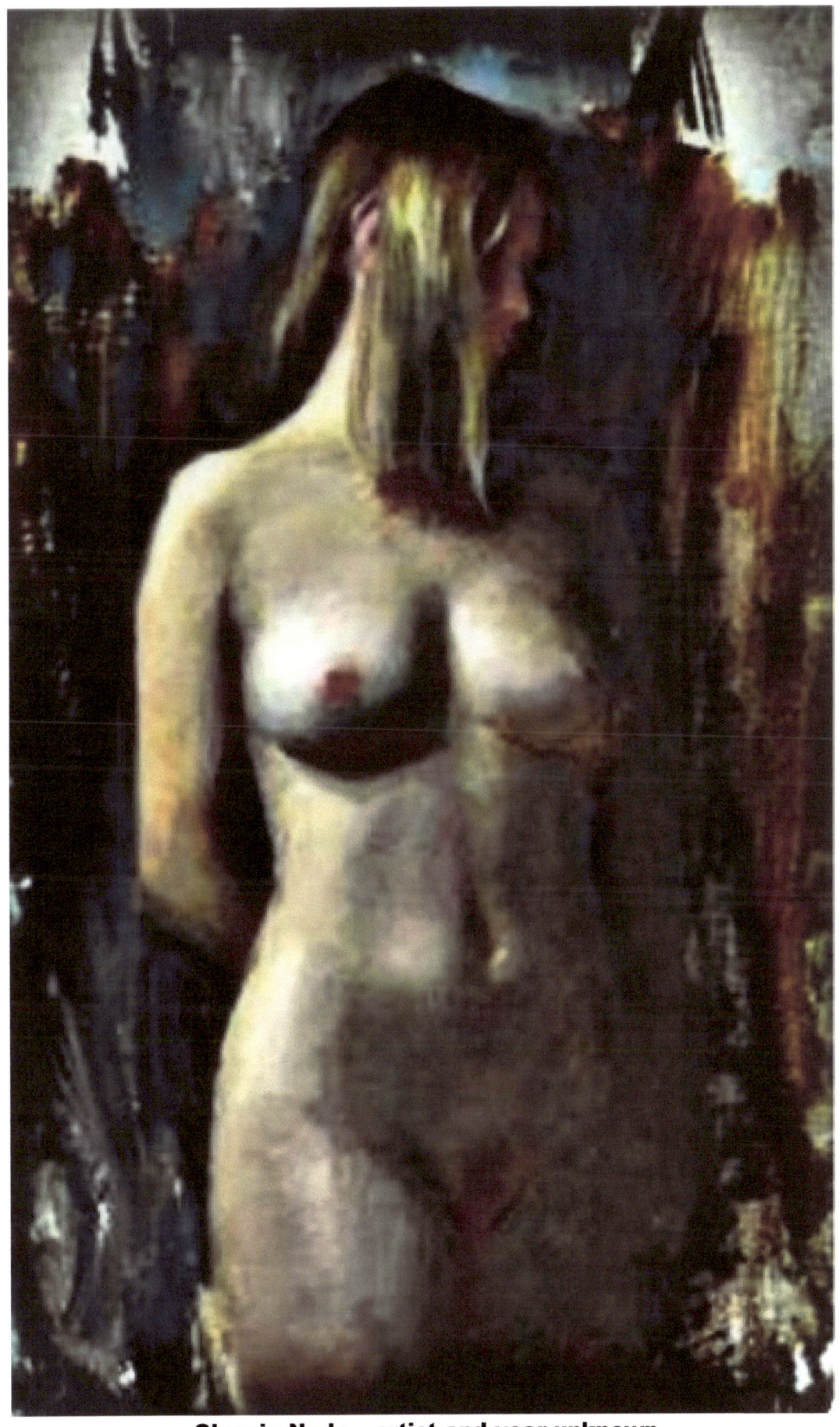

Classic Nude – artist and year unknown

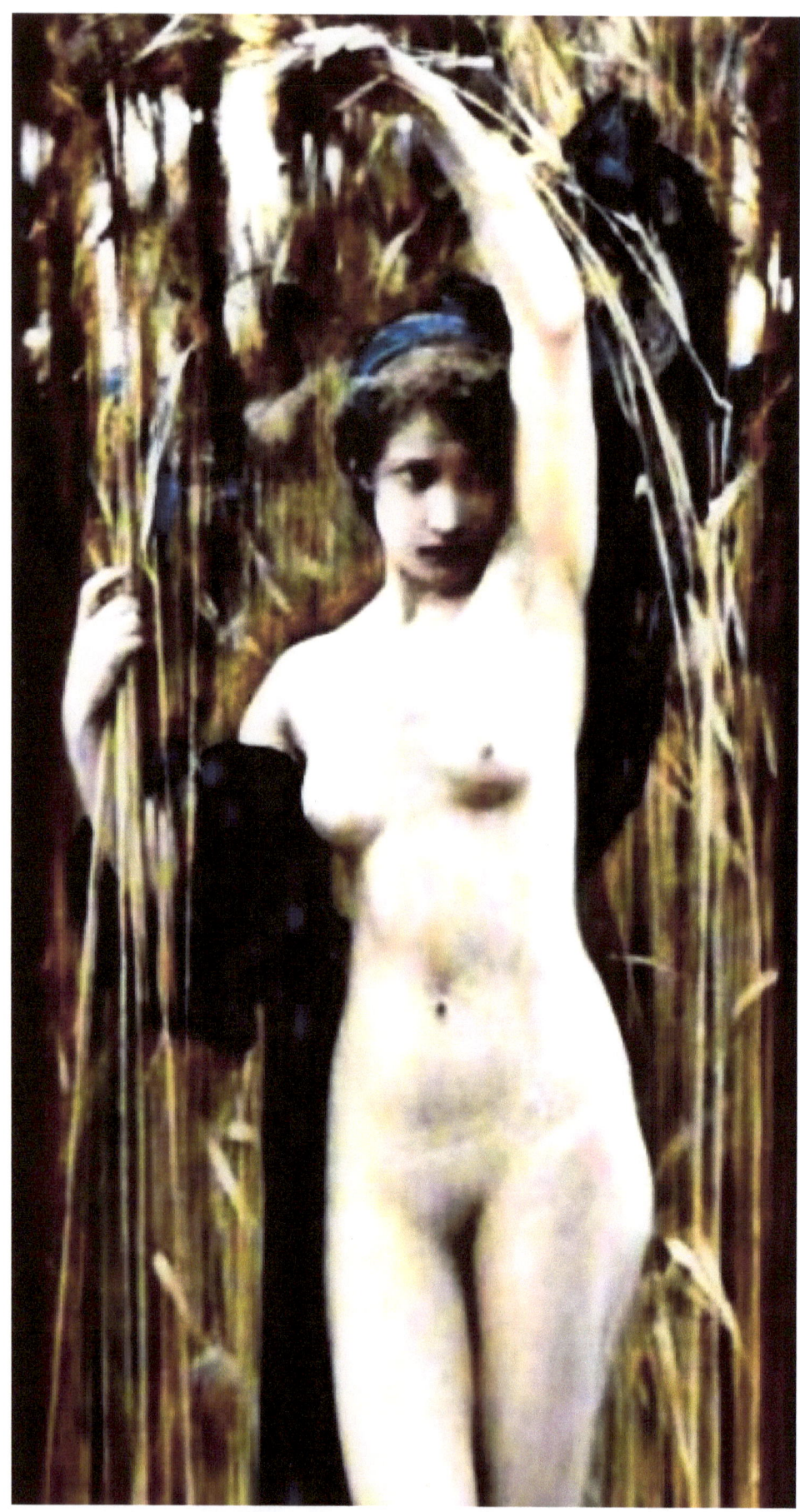

Syrinx - by Arthur Hacker, 1891

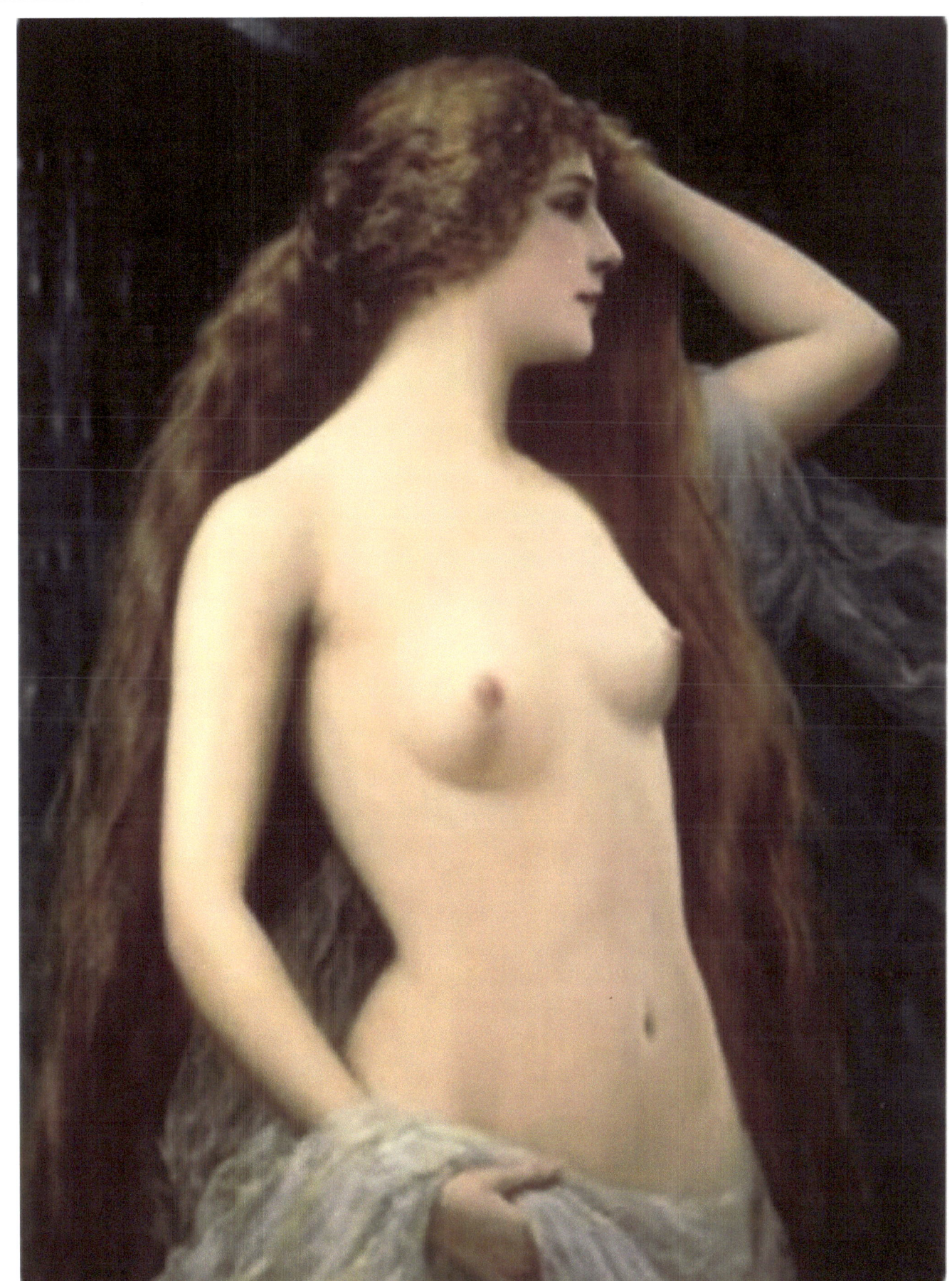

By Ignace Spiridon, 1869-1900, Italian Artist

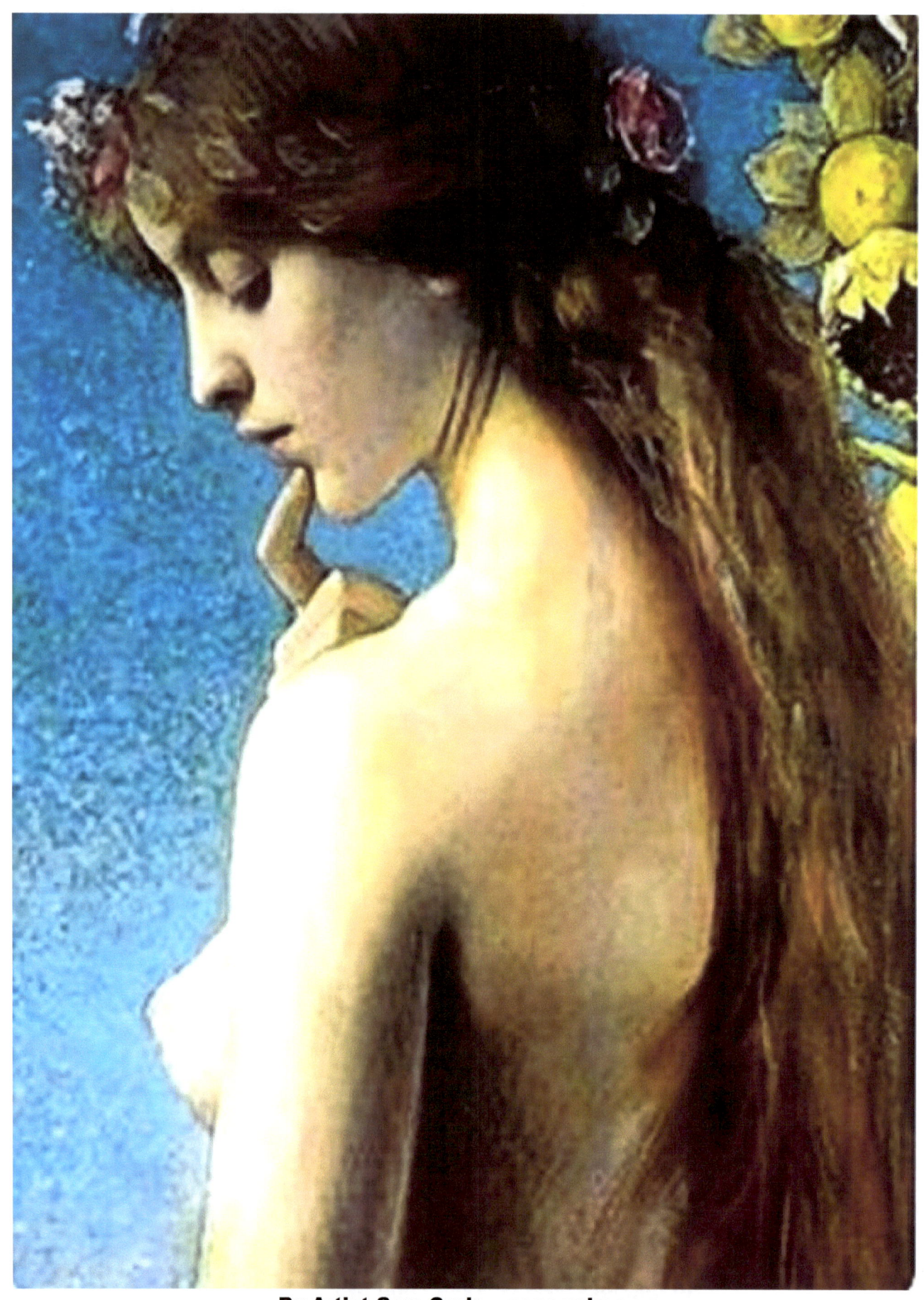

By Artist Sam Carlo – year unknown

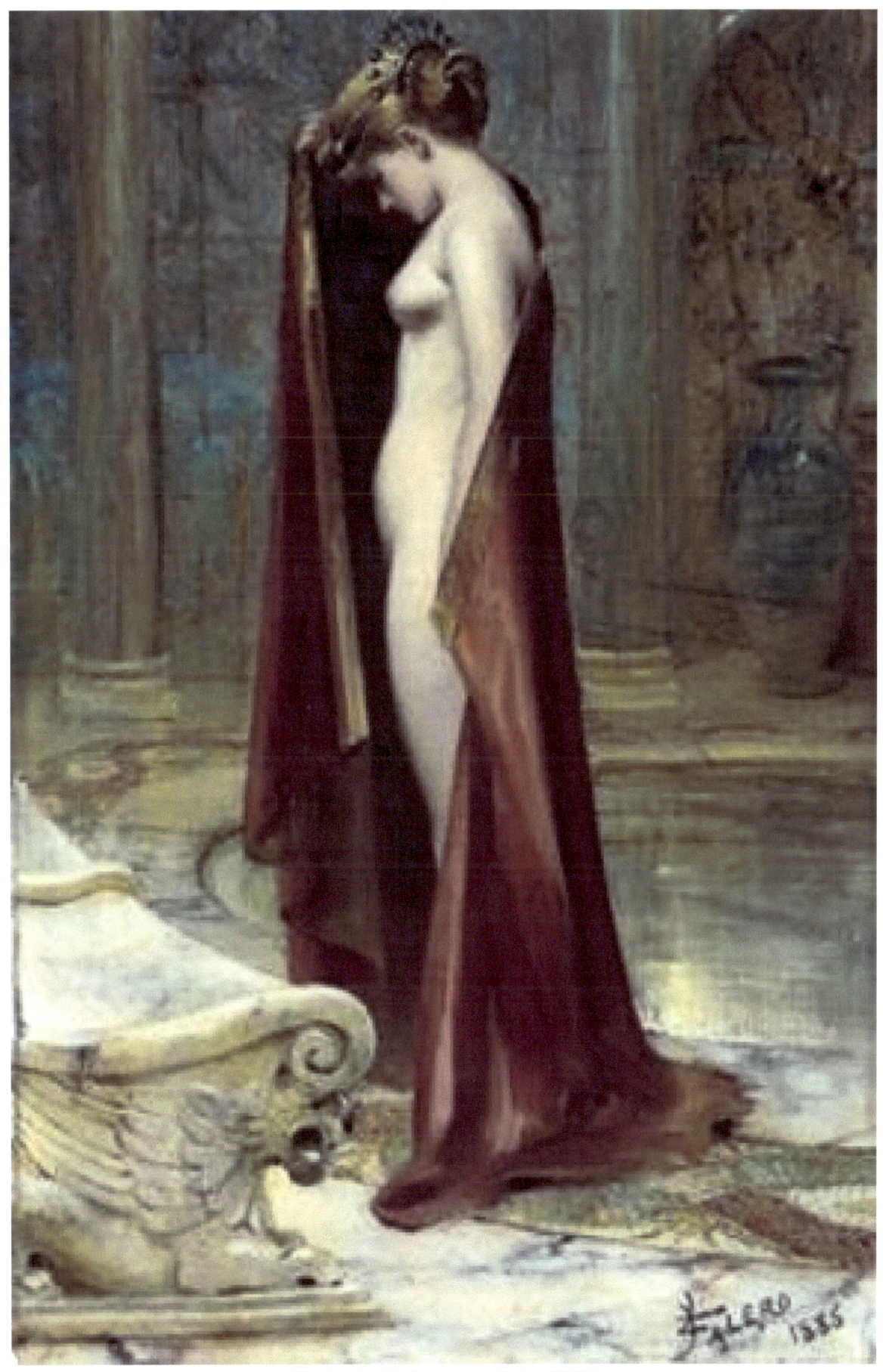

By Luis Falero, artist, 1885

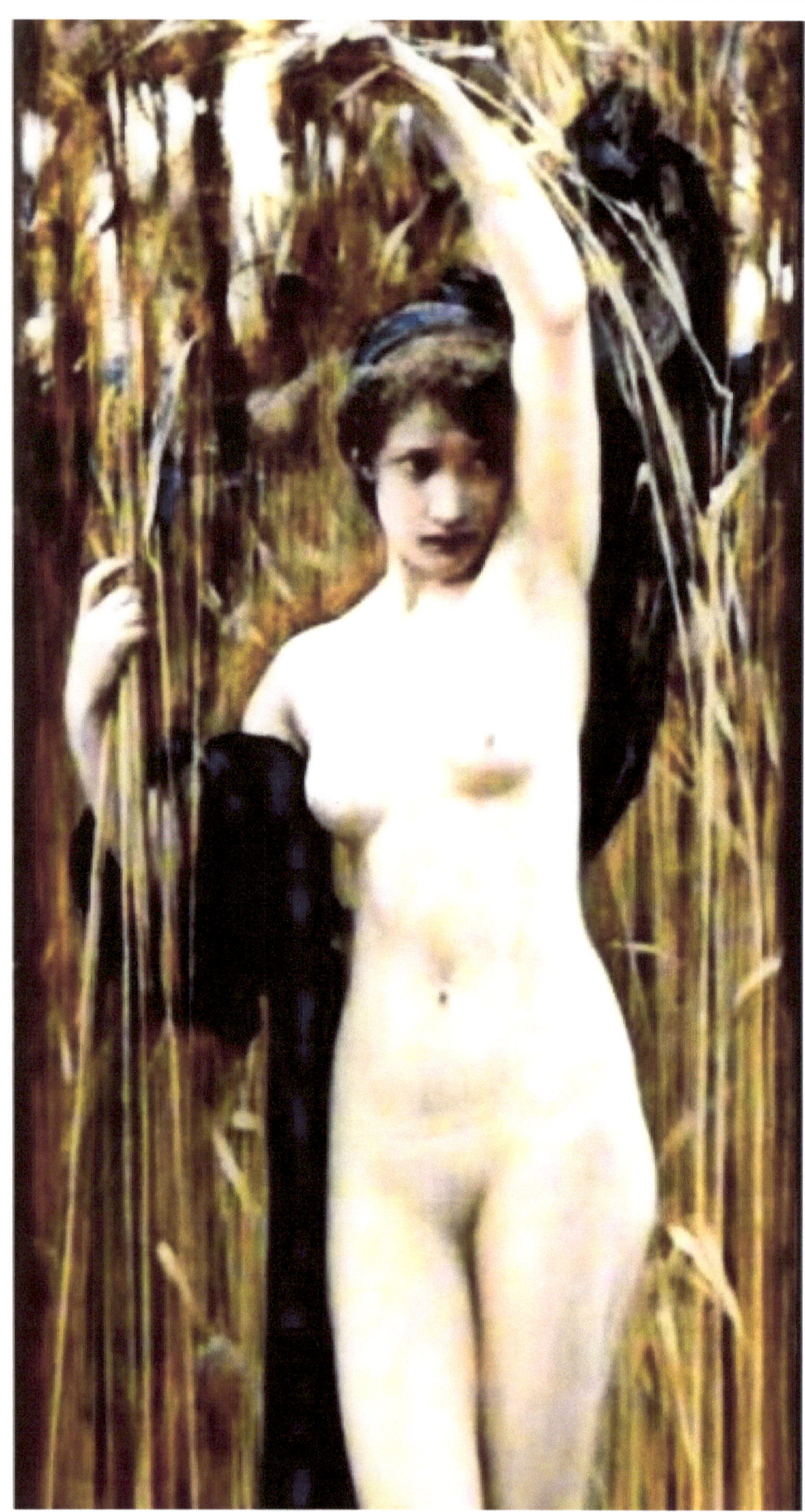

Artist and year unknown

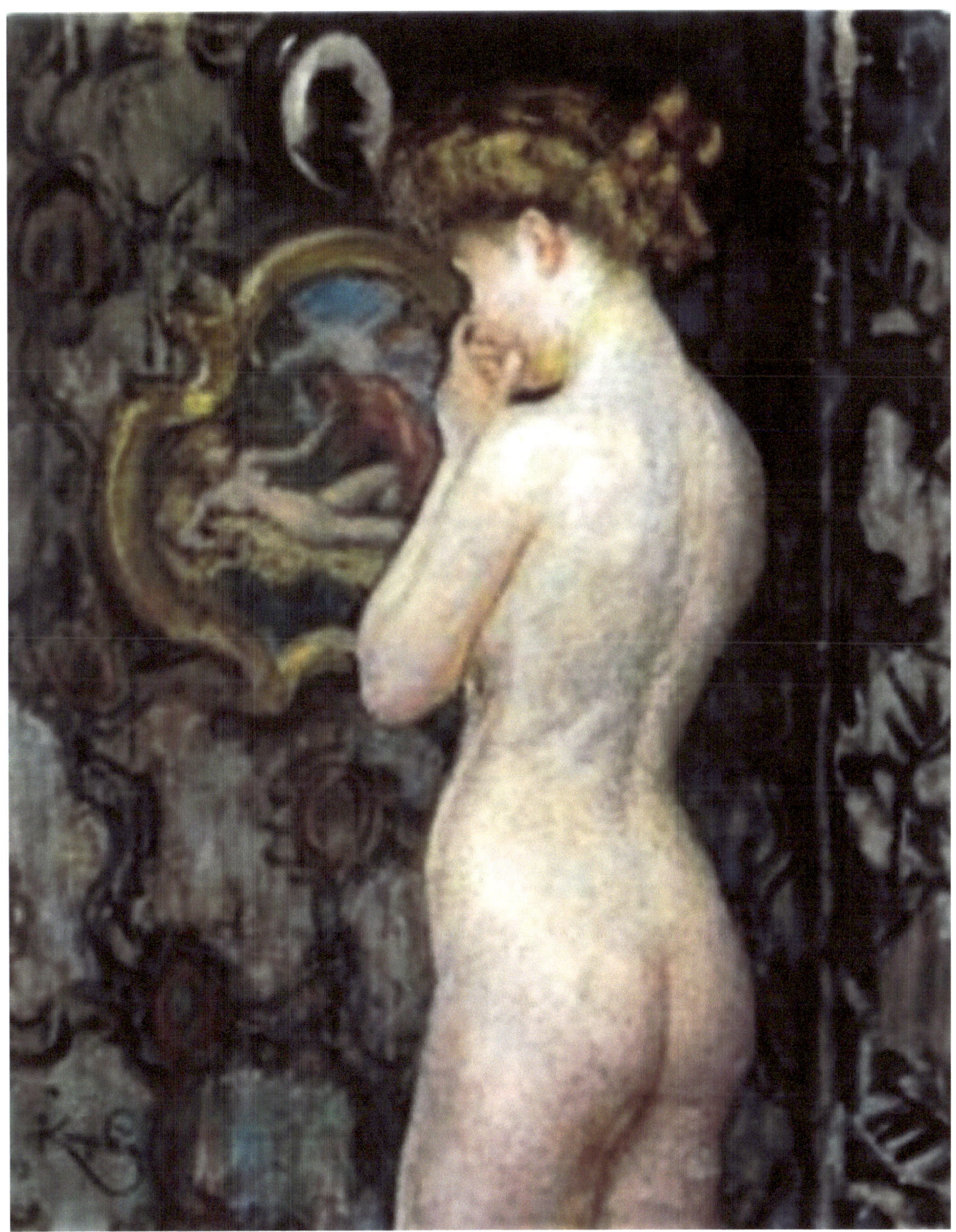

Artist and Year Unknown

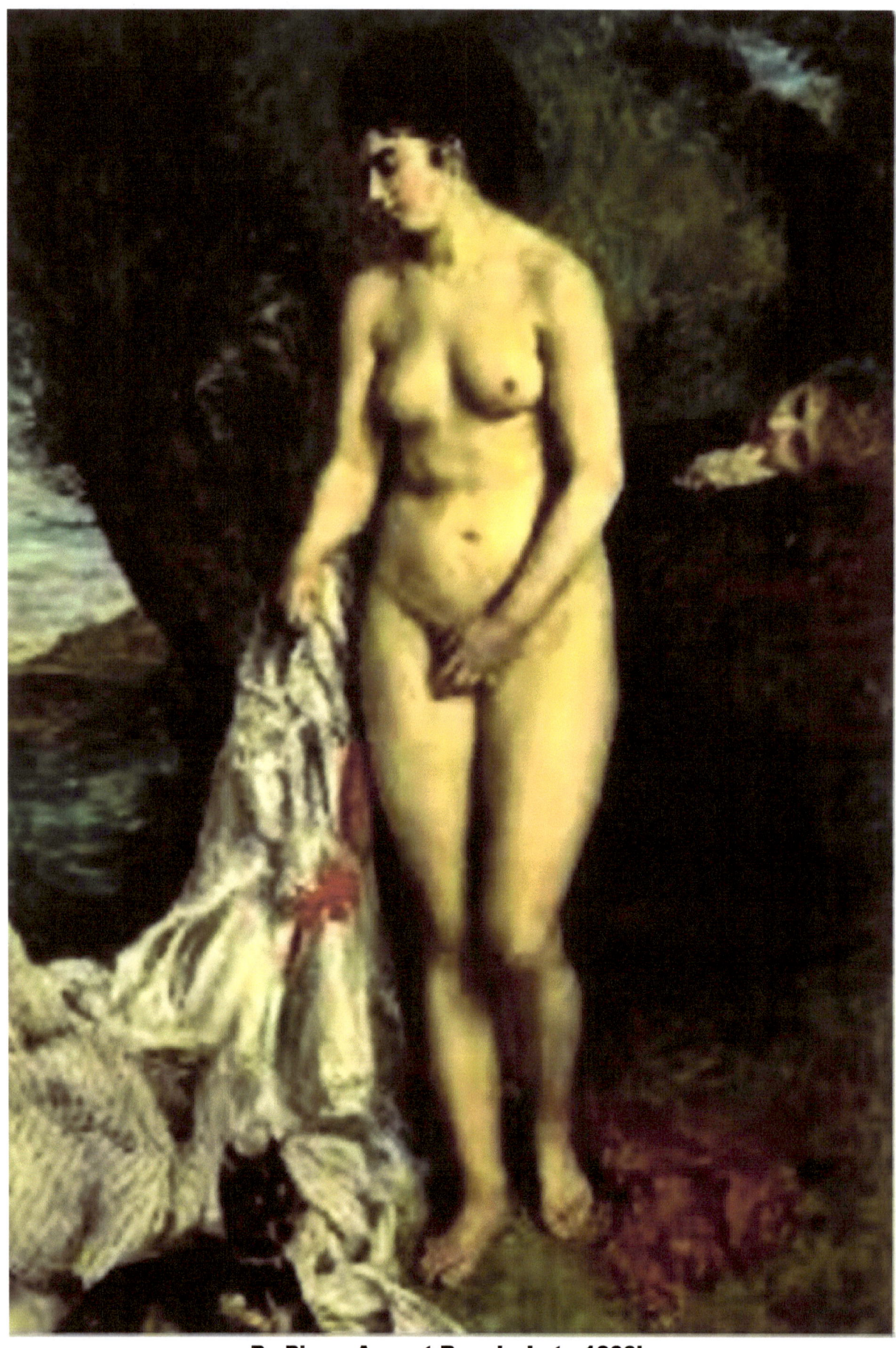

By Pierre August Renoir, Late 1800's

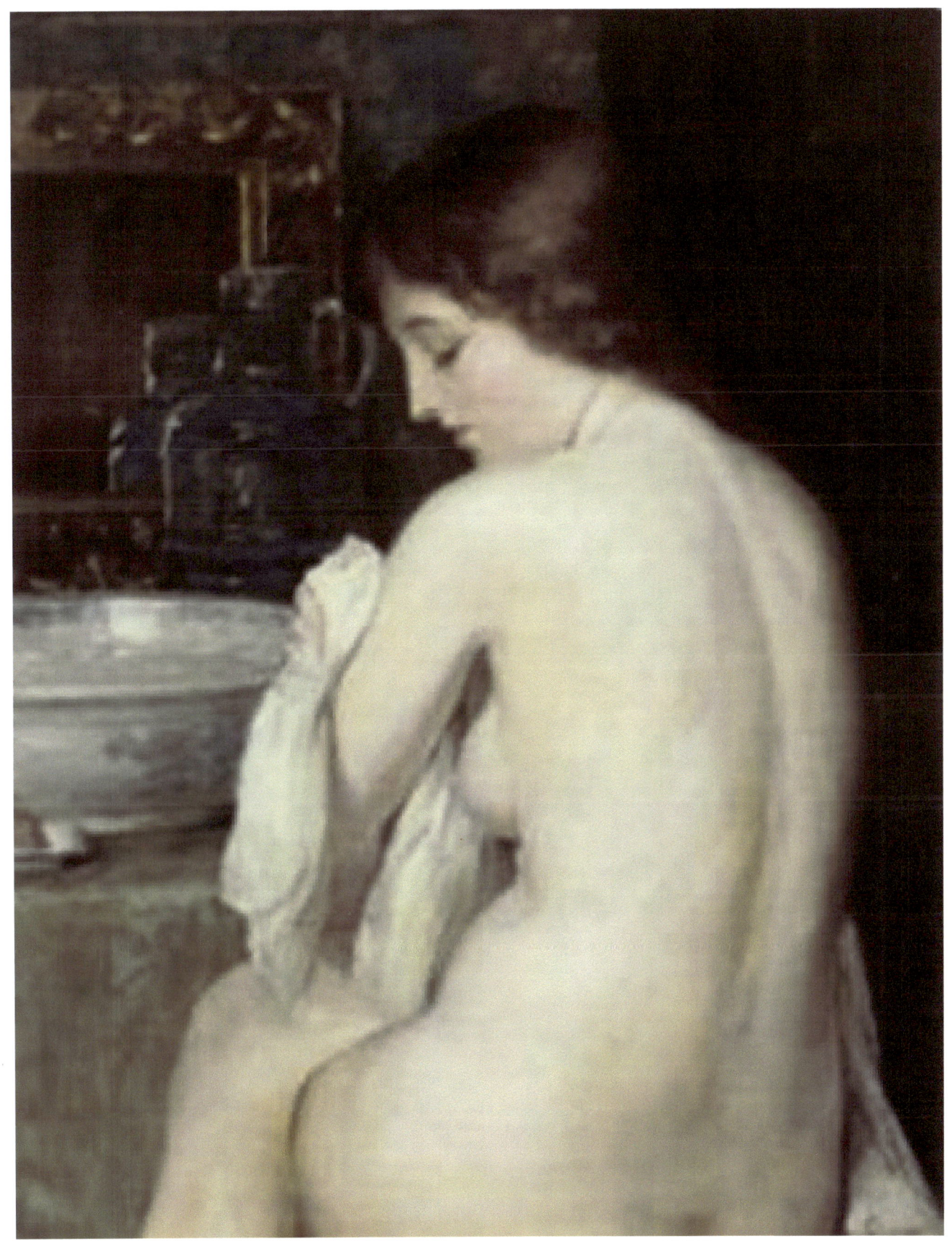

Coquetterie – by August Leveque, late 1800's

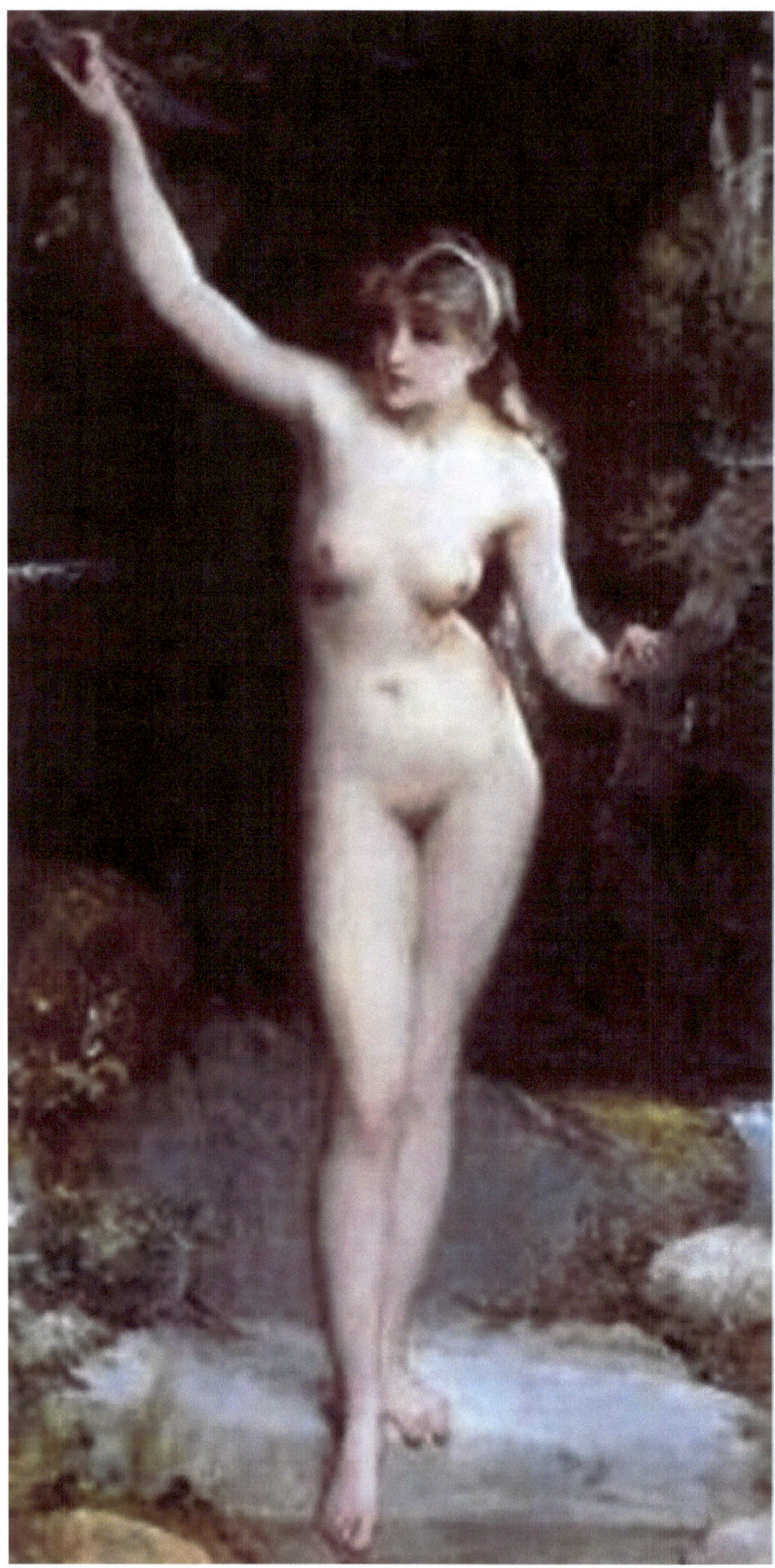

Artist and year unknown

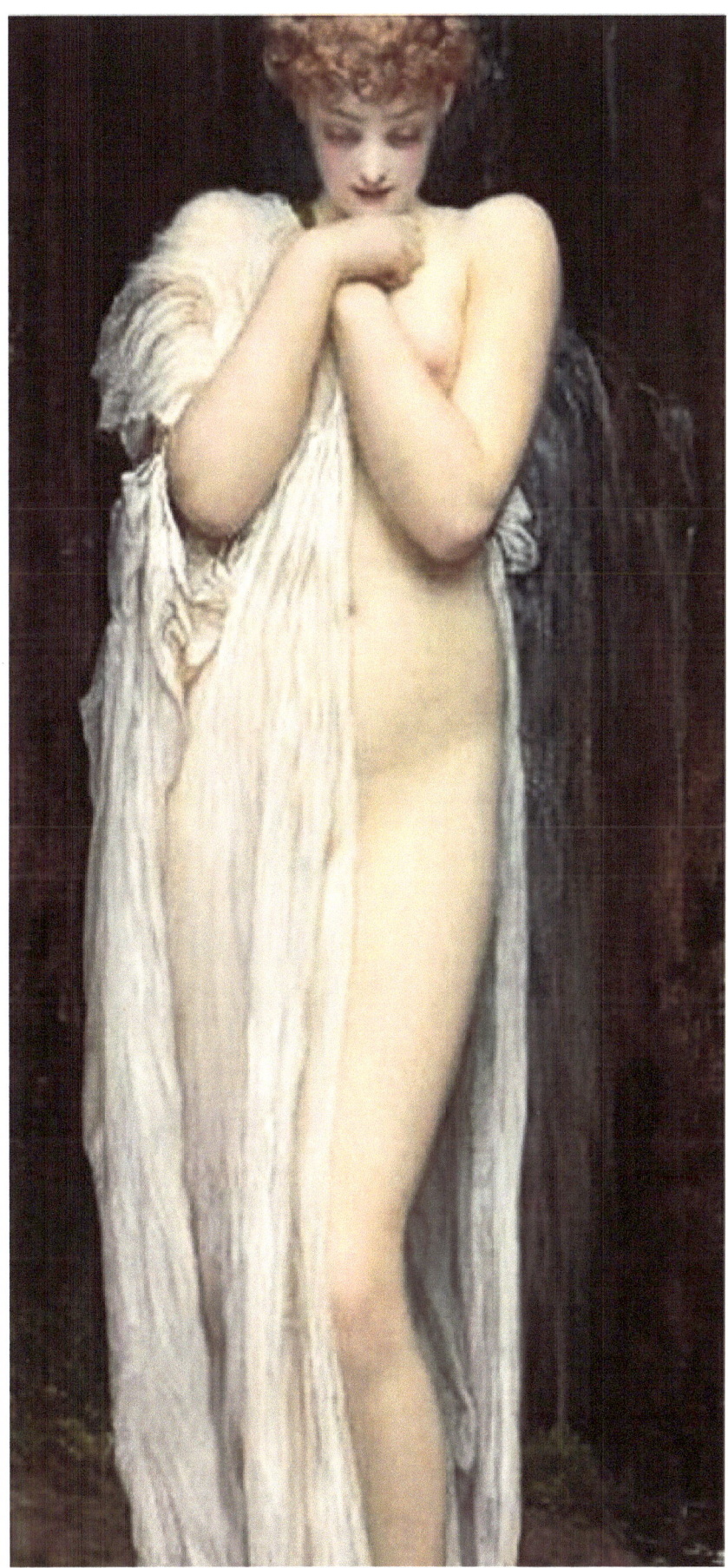

Artist and Year Unknown

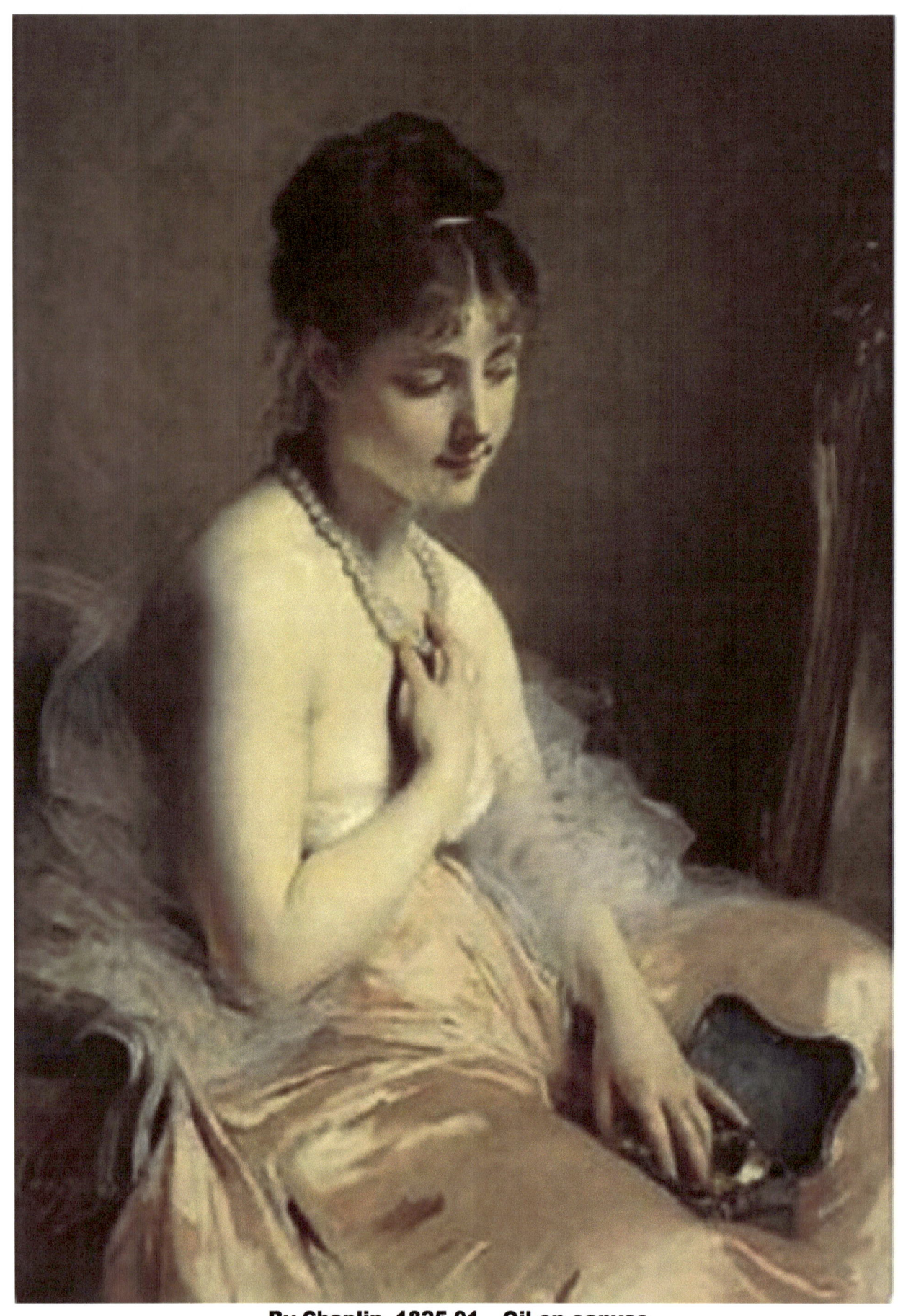

By Chaplin, 1825-91 – Oil on canvas

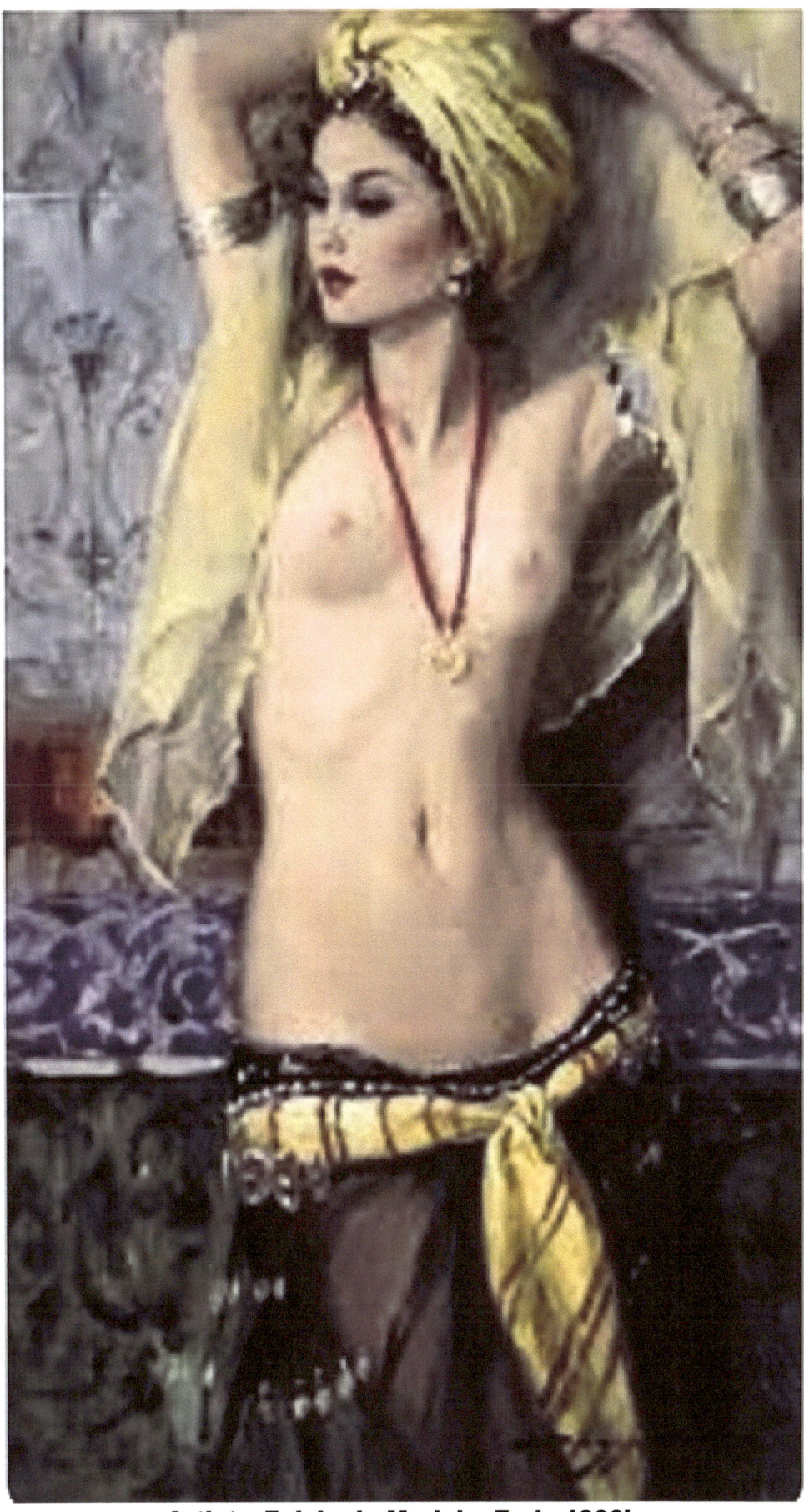

Artist – Fulvio de Marinis, Early 1900's

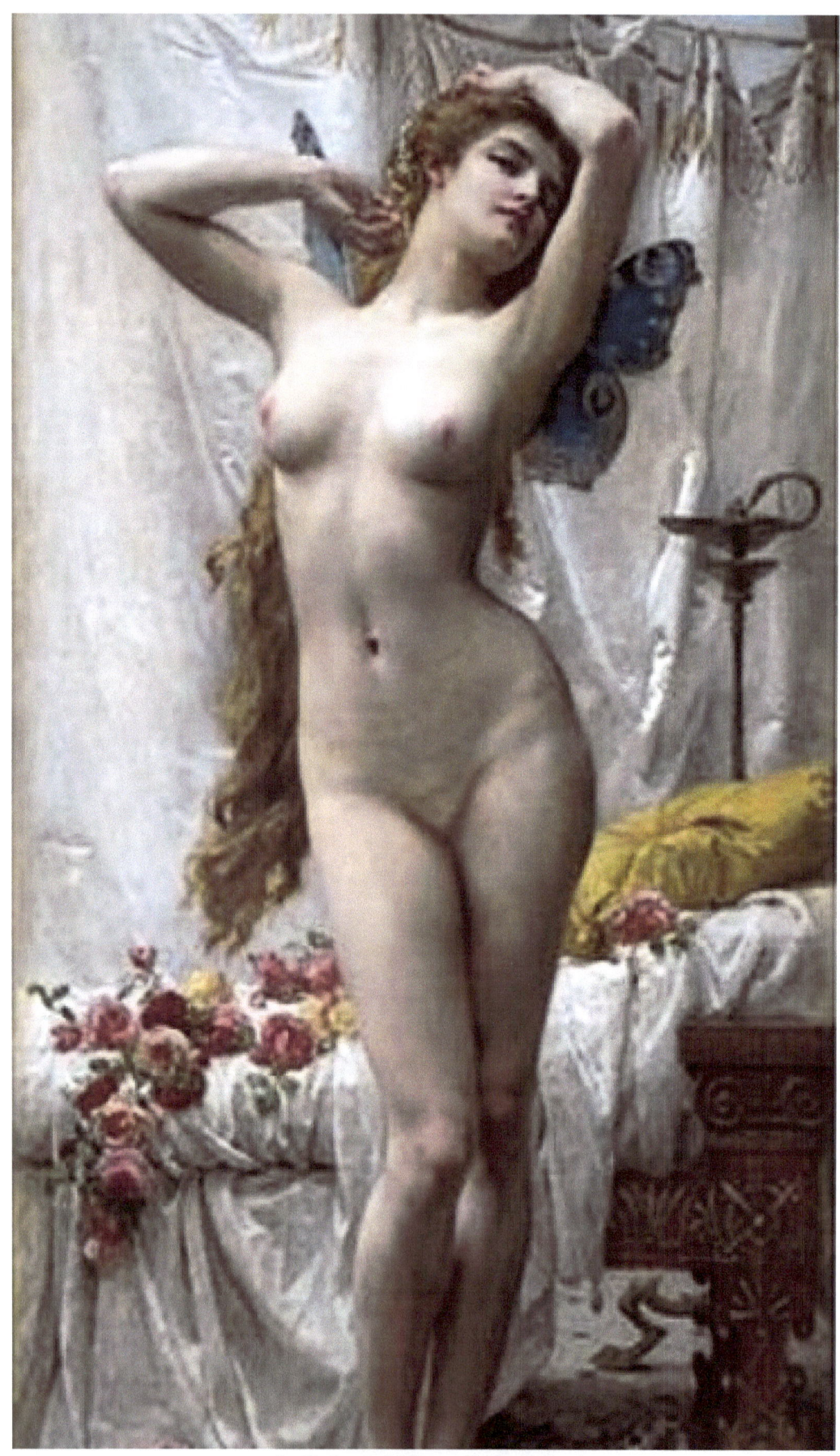

Artist and Year Unknown

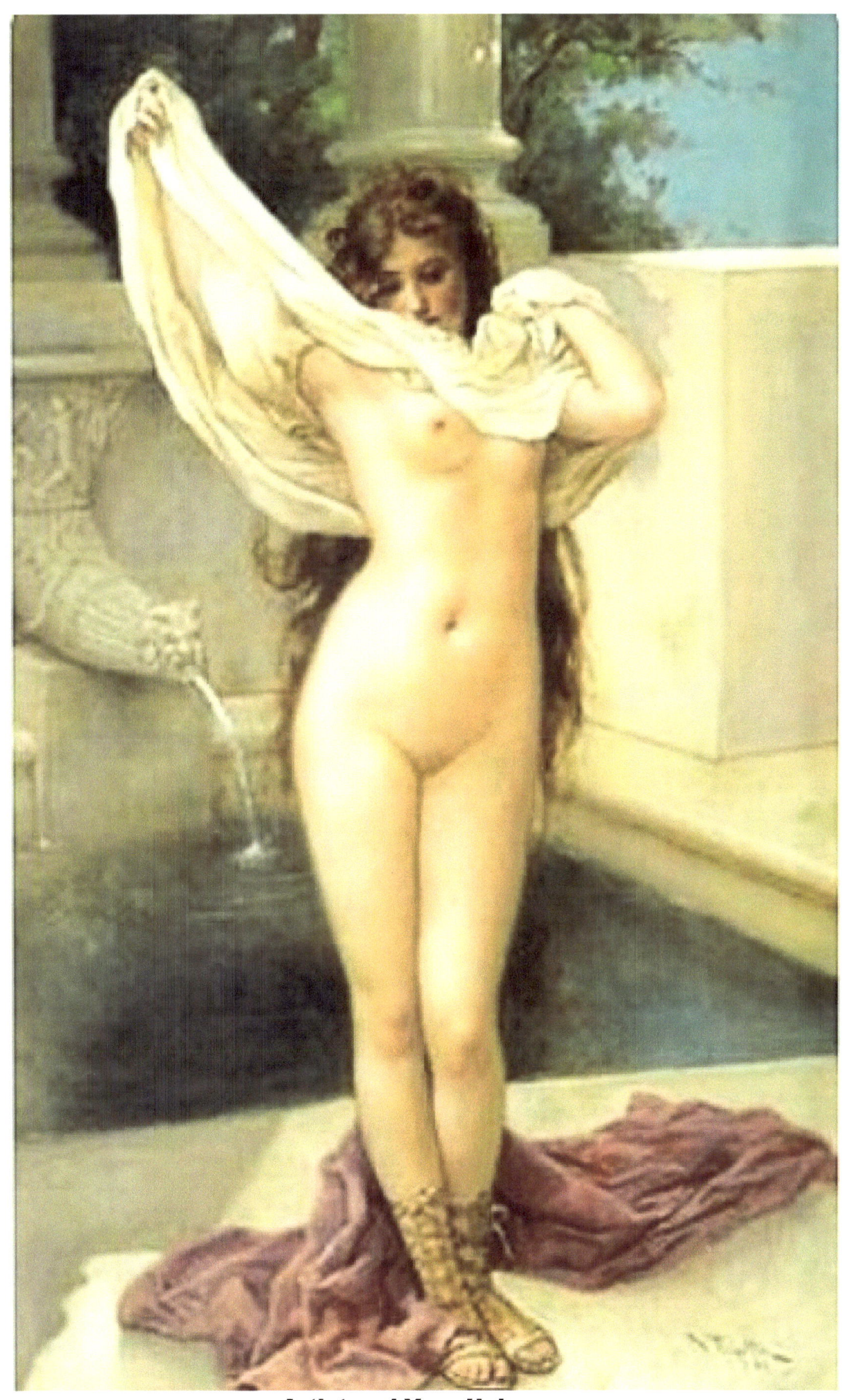

Artist and Year Unknown

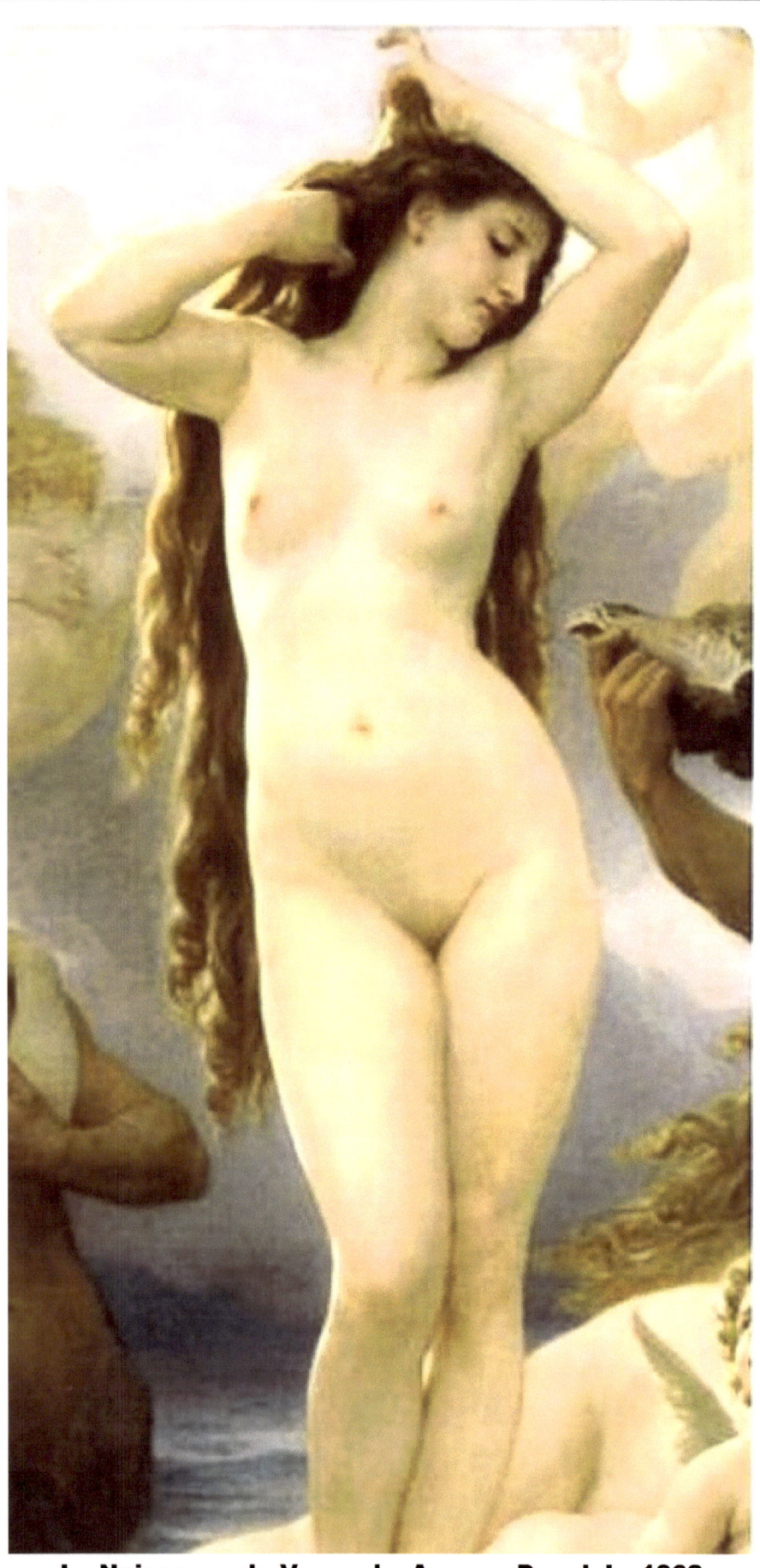

Le Naissance de Venus, by Amaury Duval Jr, 1862

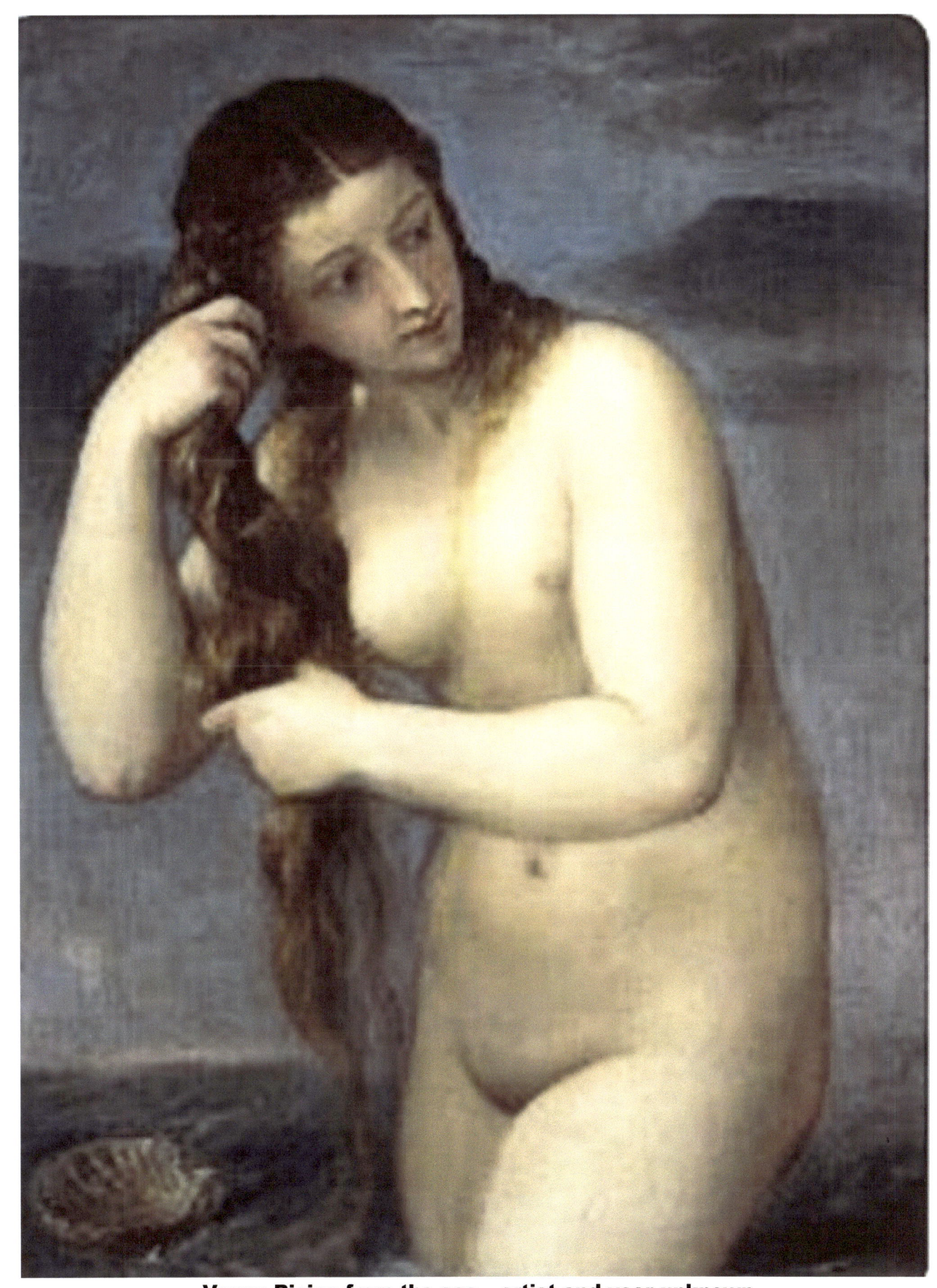

Venus Rising from the sea – artist and year unknown

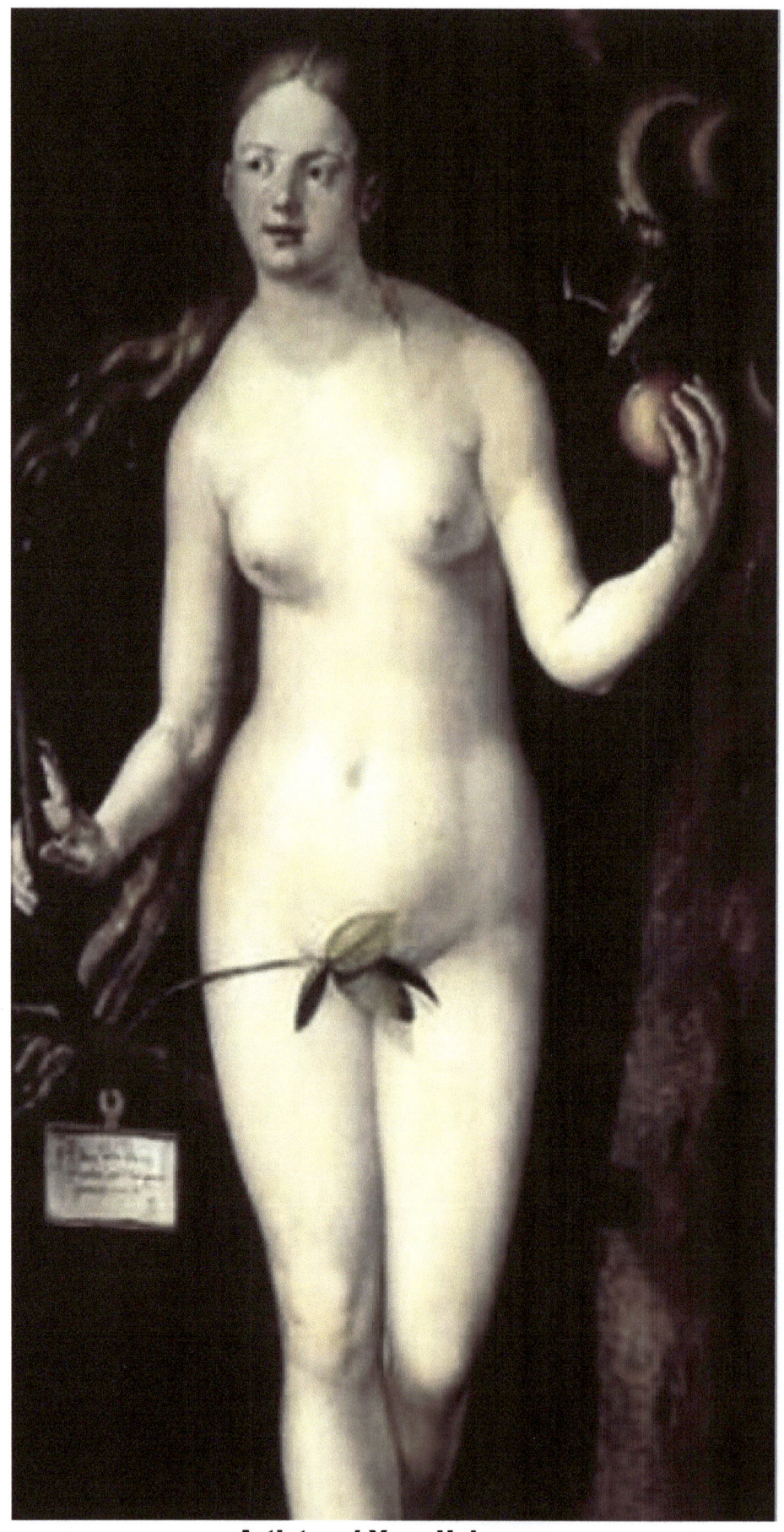

Artist and Year Unknown

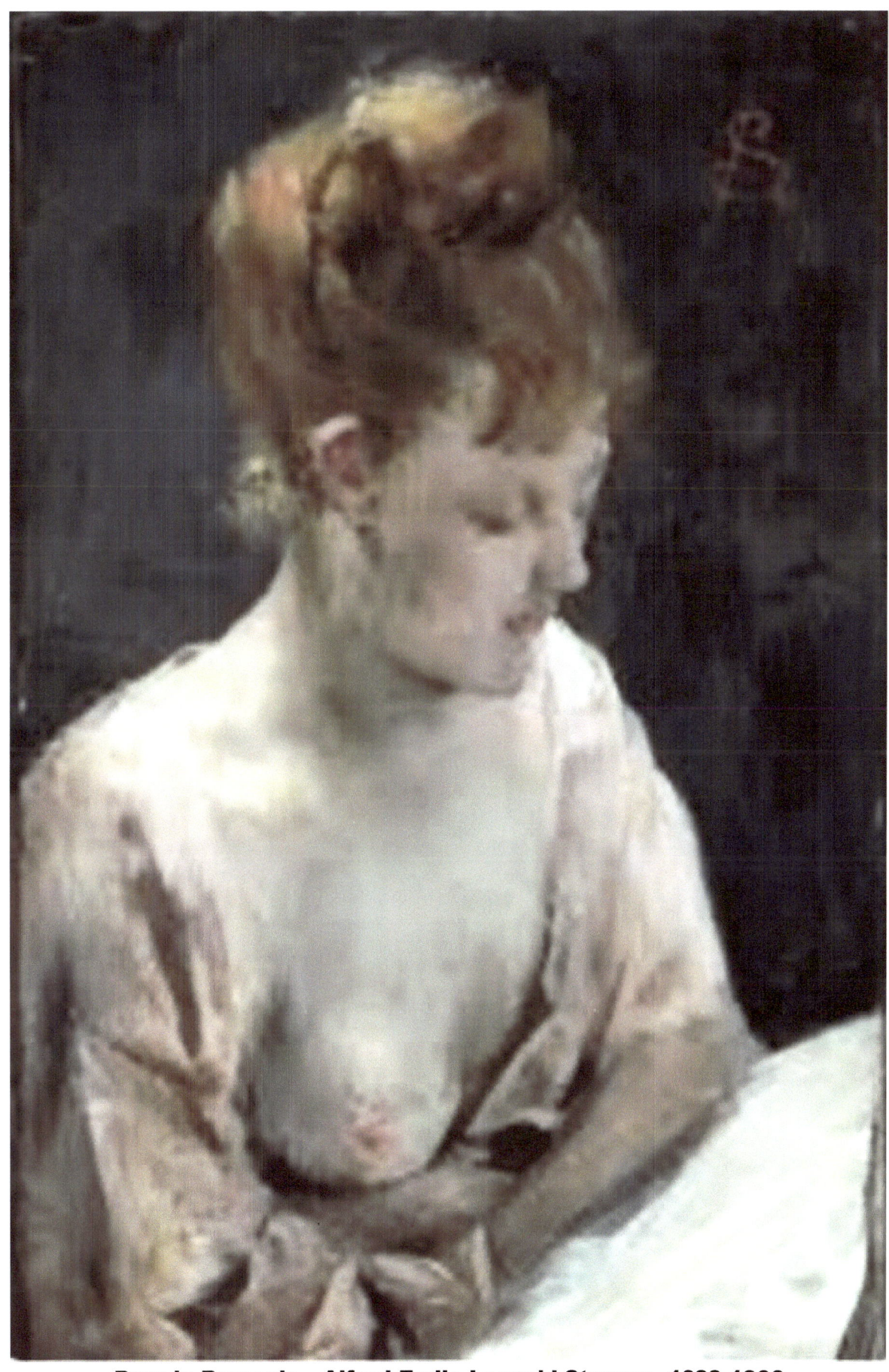

Born in Brussels – Alfred Emile Leopold Stevens, 1823-1906

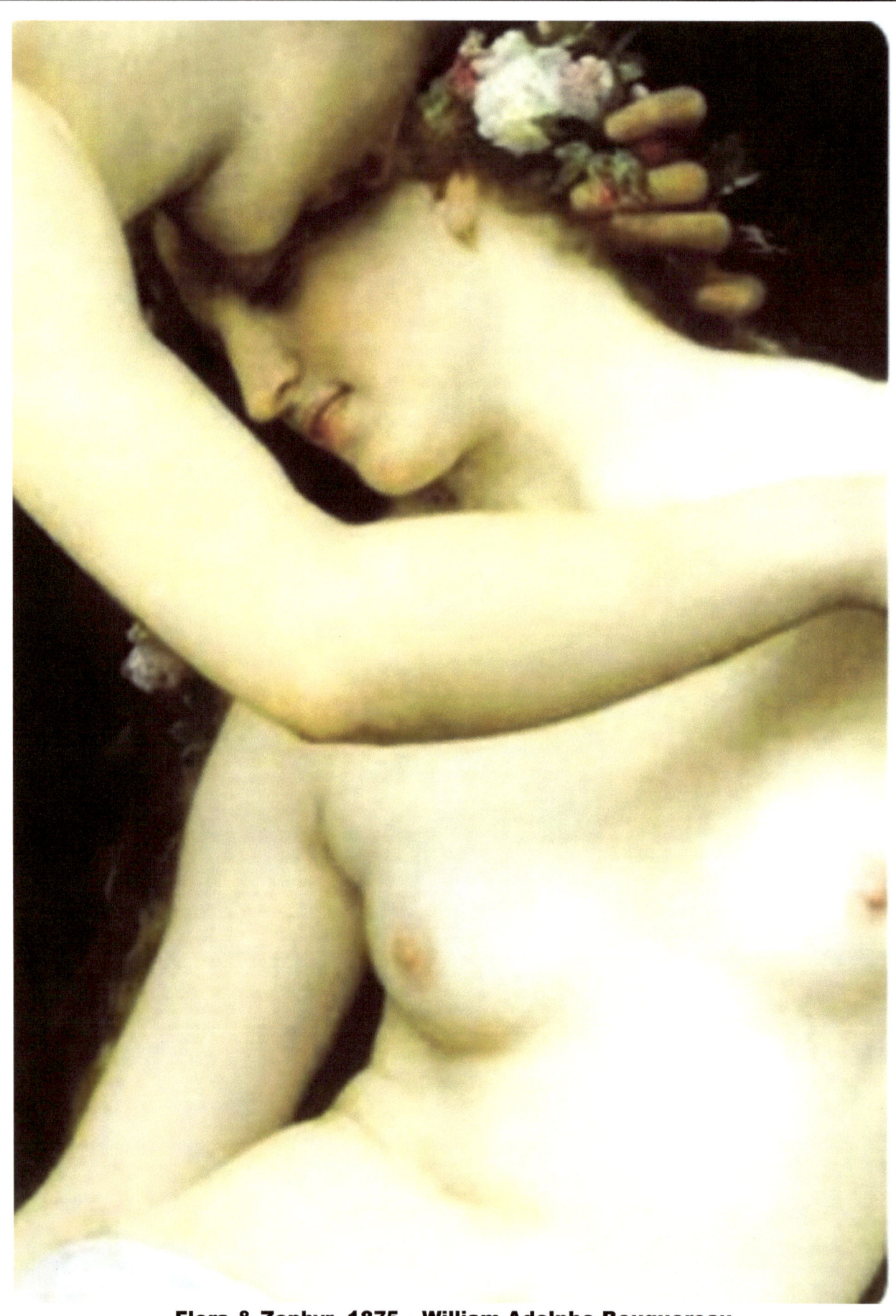

Flora & Zephyr, 1875 – William Adolphe Bouguereau

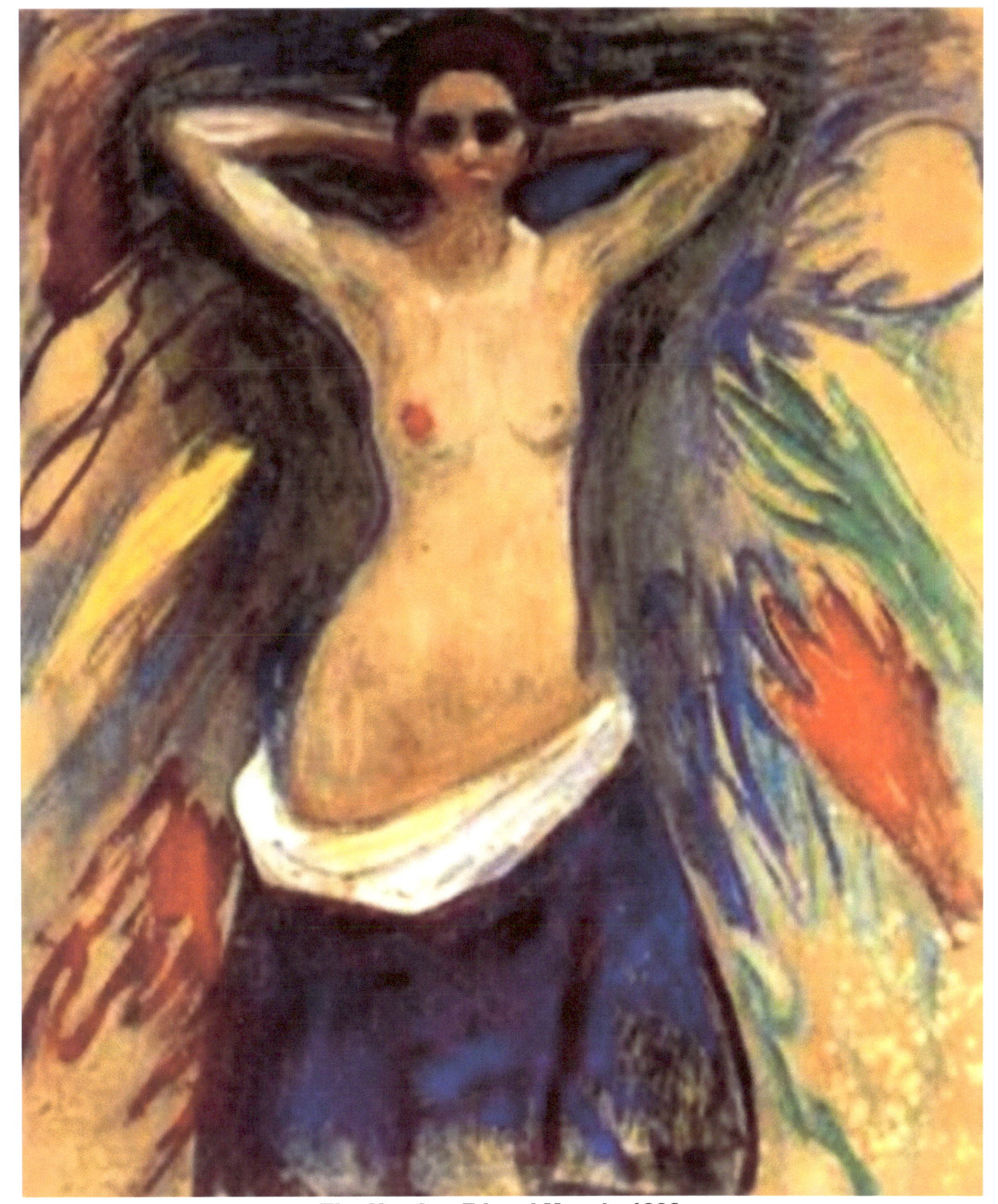

The Hands – Edvard Munch, 1893

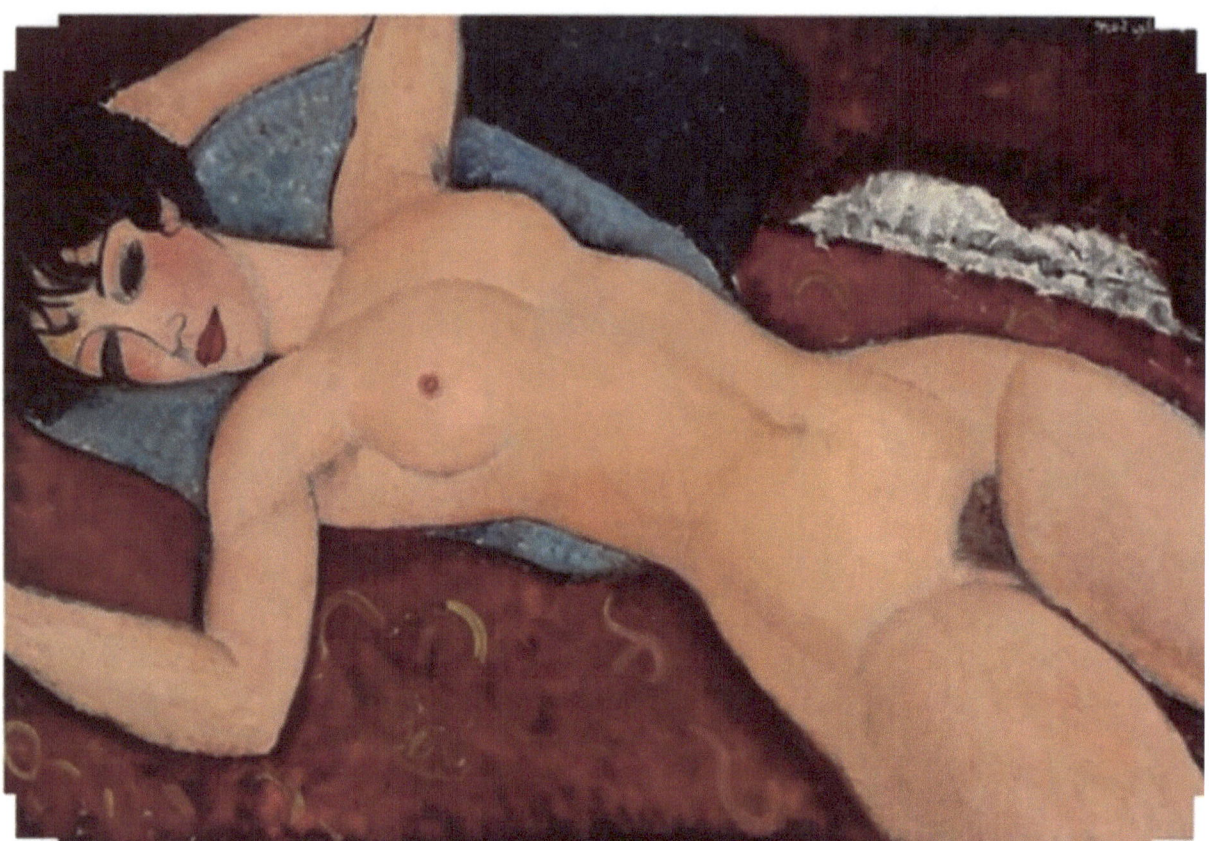

Modigliani's Nu Coche, Original sold for Eng.Pounds 115 Million

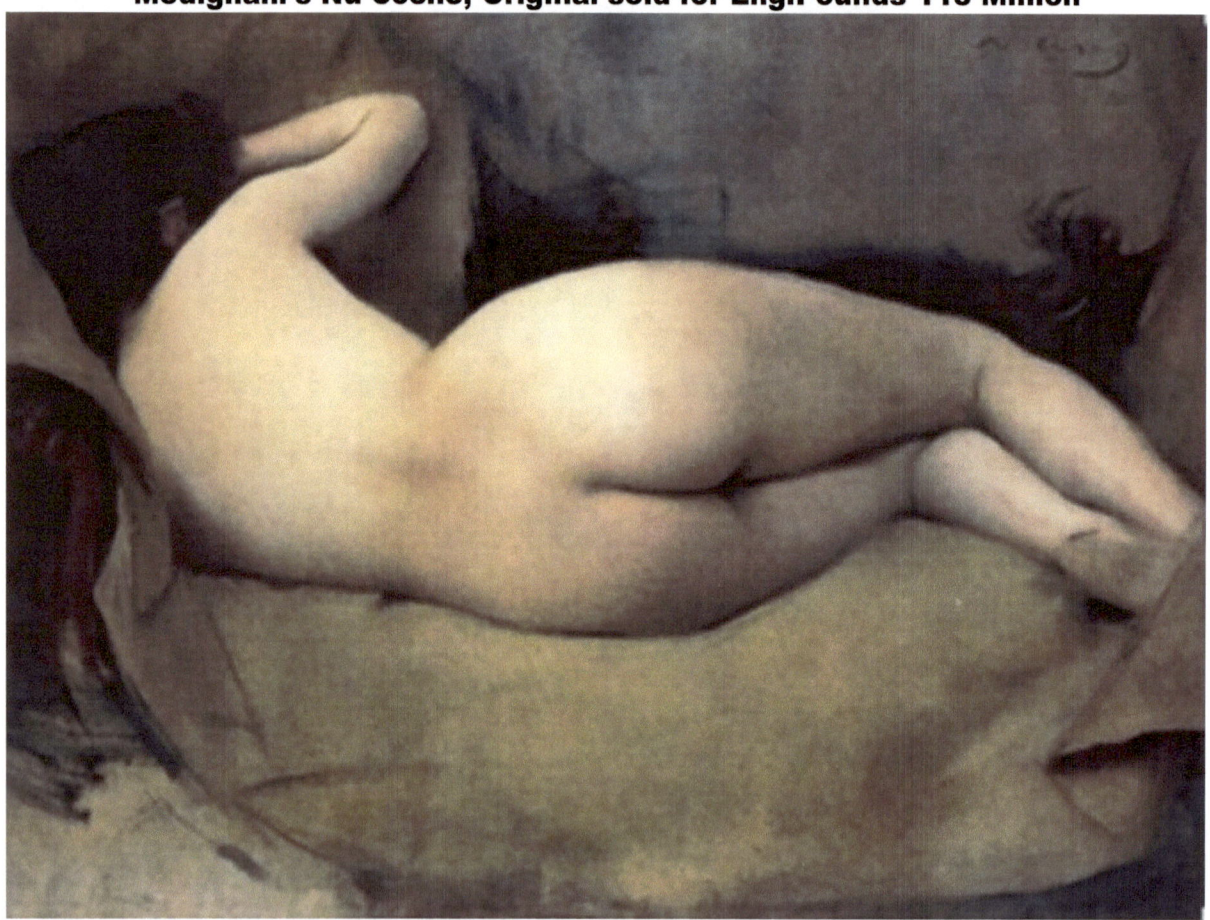

Ramon Casa y Carbo, 1894 – Figura Desnuda

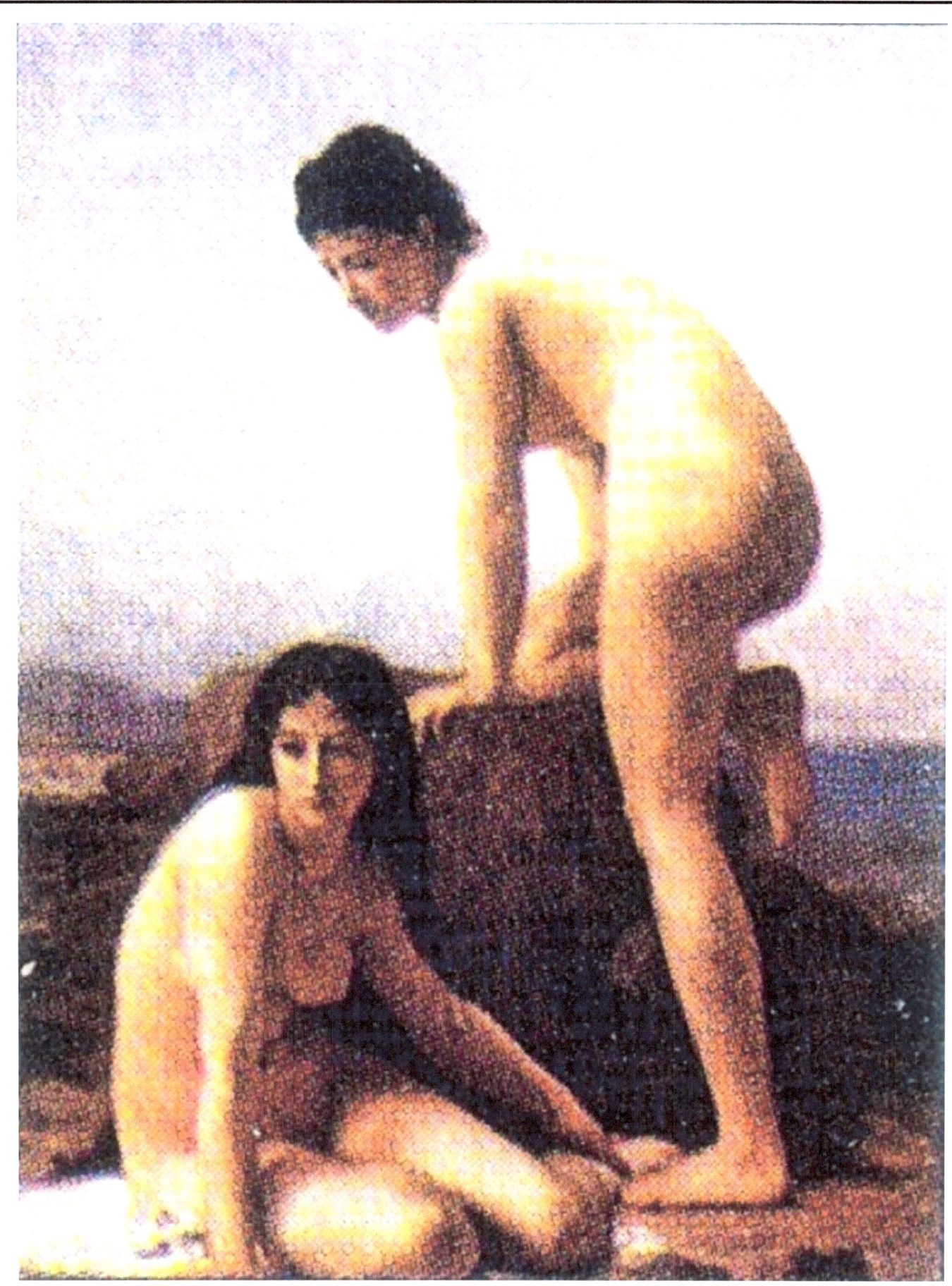

William Bouguereau – The Bathers, Lat 1800's

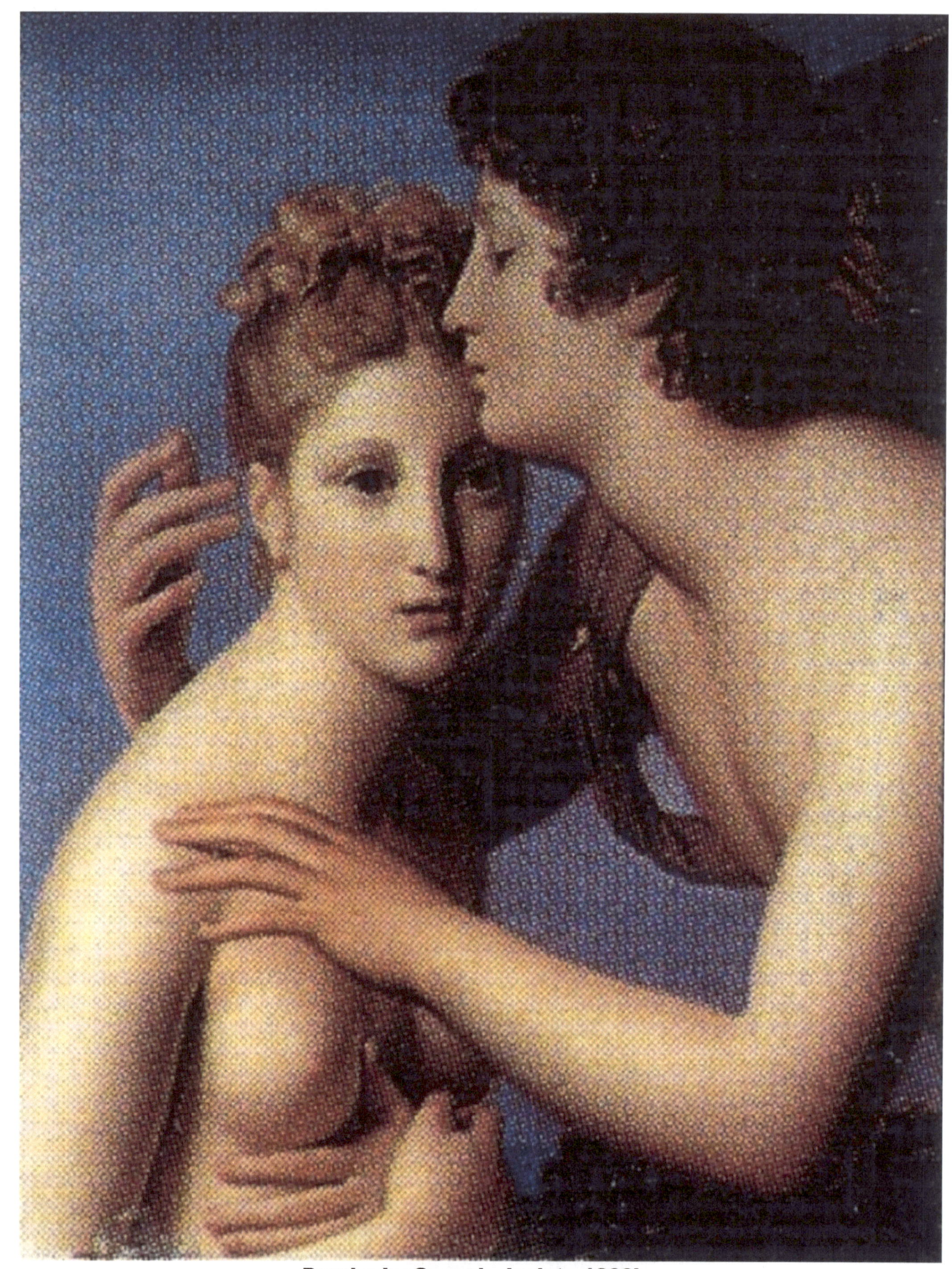

Psyche by Gerard – by lste 1800's

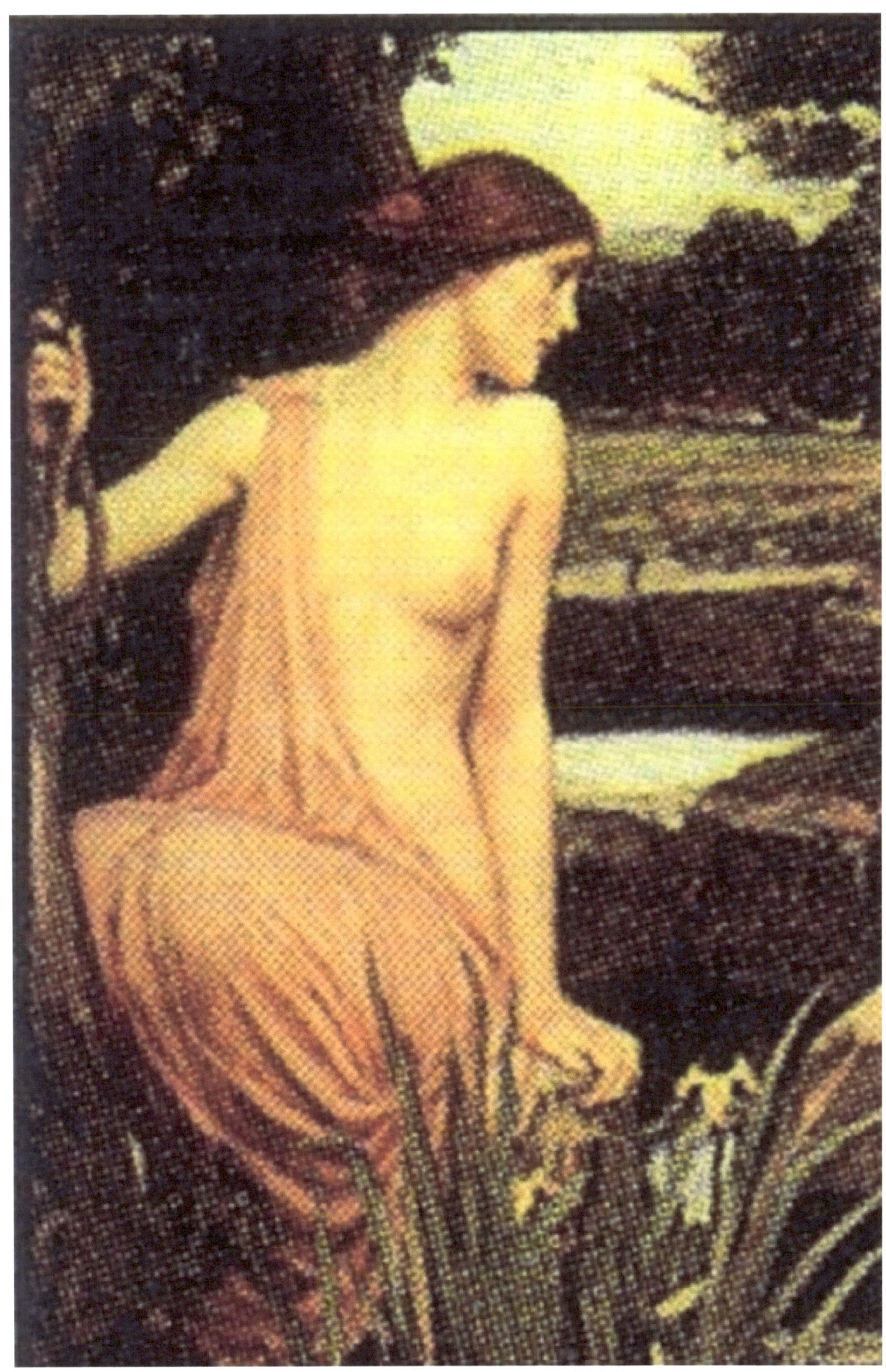

Echo - by Waterhouse, late 1800's

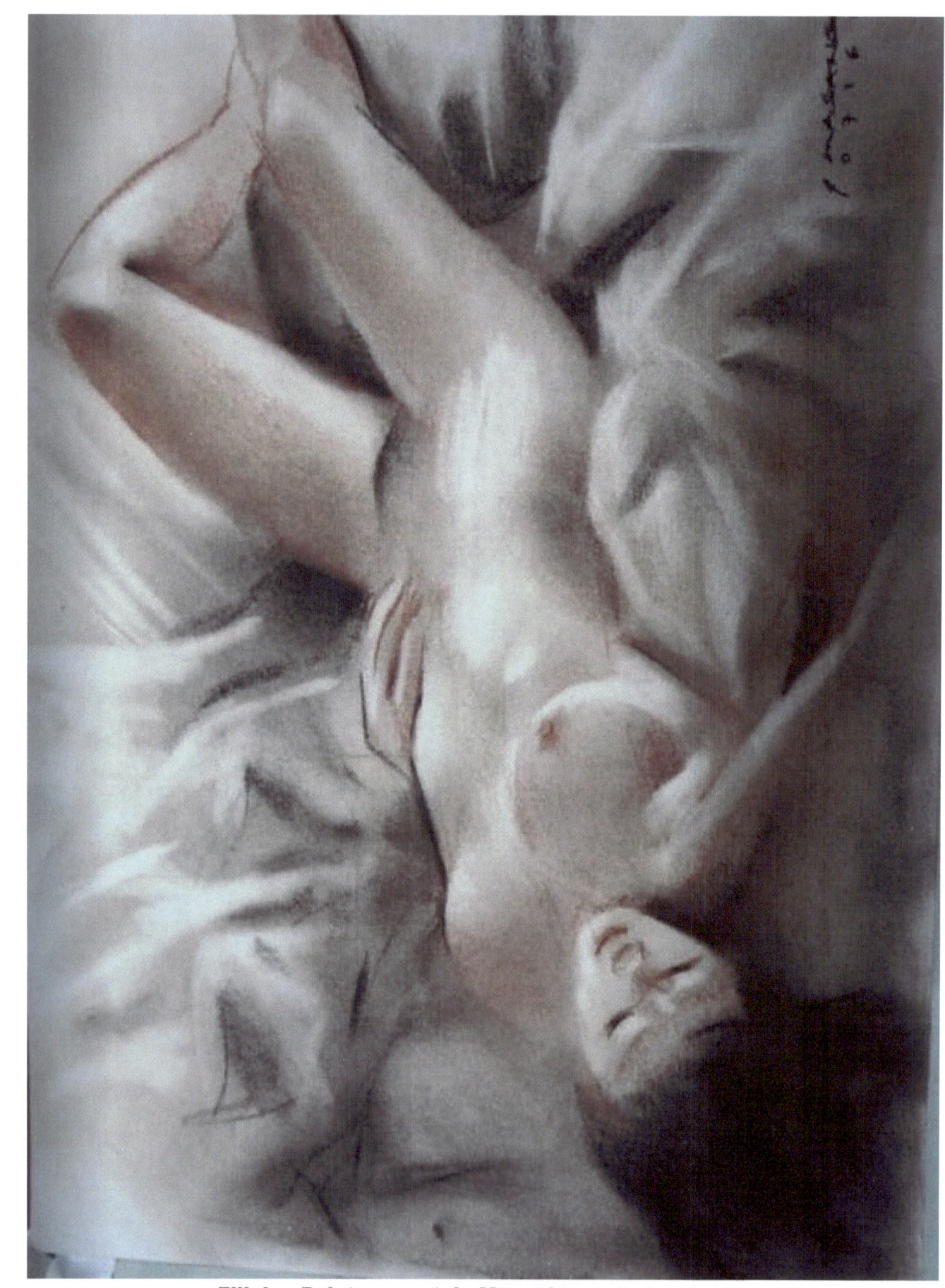

Filipino Painter – certain Masanlong, contemporary

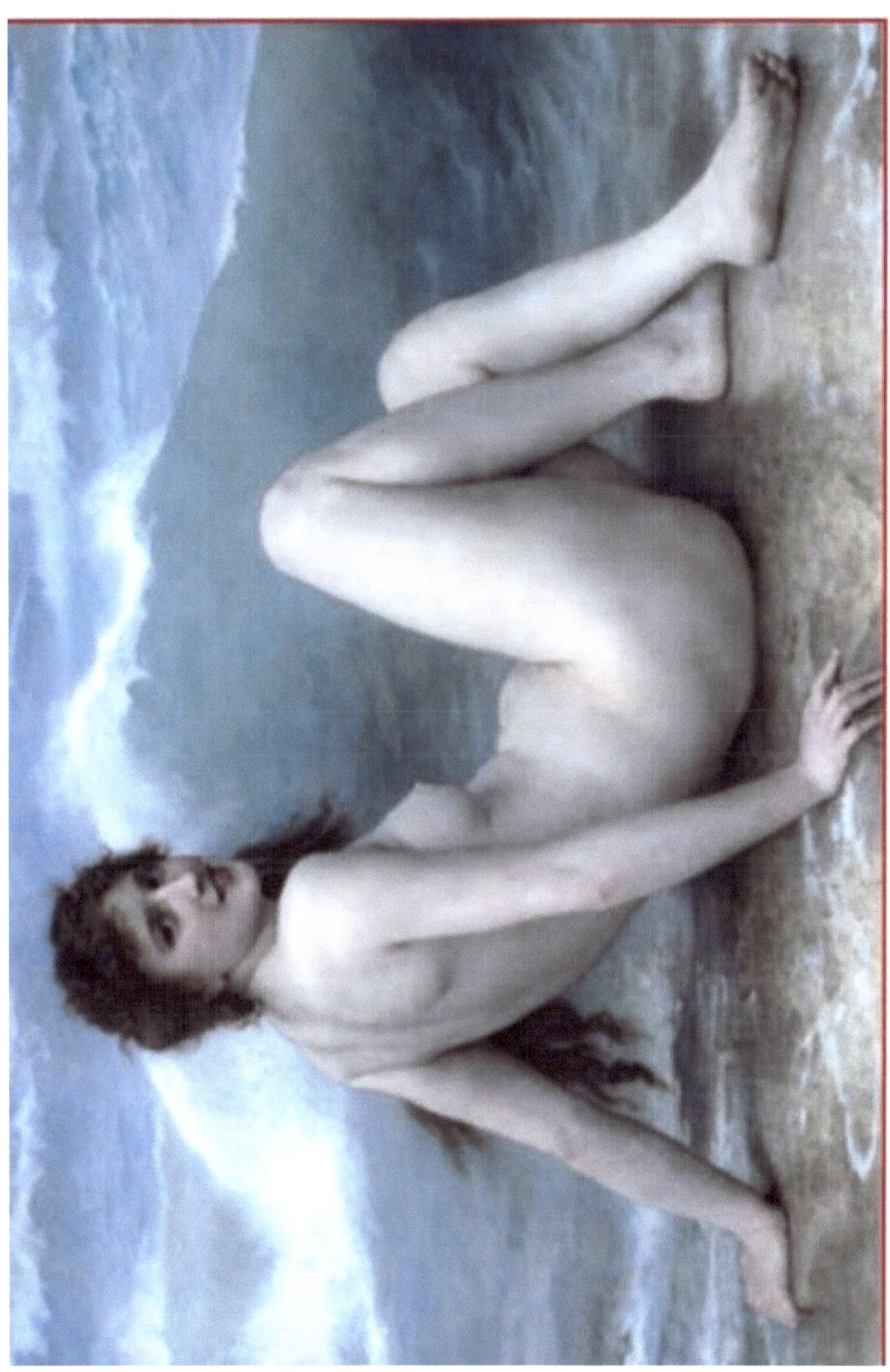

Artist & Year Unknown, contemporary painting

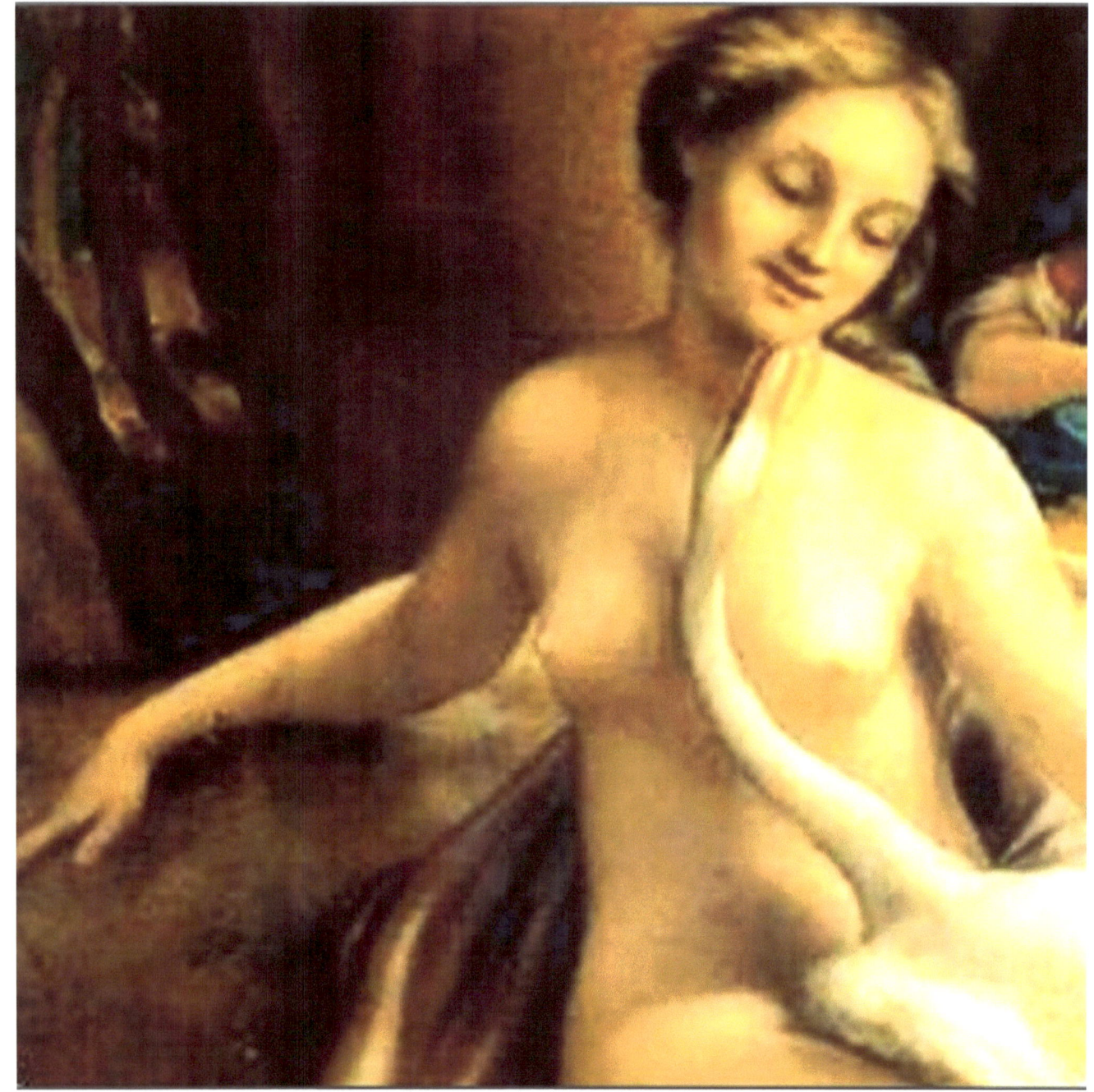

Ledda and The Swan – by Corregio, 1532

THANK YOU! We hope you enjoy this Fave Art-9 album collection of classic paintings. Most art works are copied from the internet, posters, pictures and books. Most are collector's items and can be seen in famous galleries and private homes. The originals are very expensive but copies are available from some dealers. You may display this book as coffee table book in your living room, as conversation piece. You may give this as gift . You may cut out and frame each page. Each art work is 8.5x11 inches and suitable for framing, and for wall decors.

The ISBN Code Numbers of this book are:
ISBN-13: 978- 1544112435 & ISBN-10: 1544112432
Printed in USA. Free to copy by anybody. Why copy? Just buy the book.
My other books list can be accessed at:
http://tinyurl.com/mj76ccq and http://www.jobelizes6.wix.com/mysite.
My contact email is job_elizes@yahoo.com. (Tatay Jobo Elizes, Pub.)